RACIAL AND CULTURAL
DYNAMICS
IN GROUP AND
ORGANIZATIONAL LIFE

This book is dedicated to our parents, who created the foundation that gave us the motivation and endurance to write this book.

Hattie and Luther McRae

Addie Louise Short and Louis Shields

RACIAL AND CULTURAL
DYNAMICS
IN GROUP AND
ORGANIZATIONAL LIFE

CROSSING BOUNDARIES

MARY B. McRAE
New York University

ELLEN L. SHORT
Long Island University

Los Angeles | London | New Delhi
Singapore | Washington DC

For information:

SAGE Publications, Inc.
2455 Teller Road
Thousand Oaks,
   California 91320
E-mail: order@sagepub.com

SAGE Publications India Pvt. Ltd.
B 1/I 1 Mohan Cooperative
   Industrial Area
Mathura Road, New Delhi 110 044
India

SAGE Publications Ltd.
1 Oliver's Yard
55 City Road
London EC1Y 1SP
United Kingdom

SAGE Publications,
   Asia-Pacific Pte. Ltd.
33 Pekin Street #02-01
Far East Square
Singapore 048763

Printed in the United States of America

Library of Congress Cataloging-in-Publication Data

McRae, Mary B.
Racial and cultural dynamics in group and organizational life:
crossing boundaries/Mary B. McRae and Ellen L. Short.
      p. cm.
Includes bibliographical references and index.
ISBN 978-1-4129-3986-7 (pbk.)
   1. Race. 2. Cultural pluralism. 3. Community development. 4. Communication in community development. I. Short, Ellen L. II. Title.

HT1521.M377 2010
302.3—dc22   2009021458

This book is printed on acid-free paper.

10   11   12   13   10   9   8   7   6   5   4   3   2

Acquisitions Editor:	Kassie Graves
Editorial Assistant:	Veronica Novak
Production Editor:	Carla Freeman
Copy Editor:	QuADS Prepress (P) Ltd.
Typesetter:	C&M (P) Digitals Ltd.
Proofreader:	Theresa Kay
Indexer:	Diggs Publication Services
Cover Designer:	Gail Buschman
Marketing Manager:	Stephanie Adams

Contents

Introduction

Basic Conceptual Framework of the Book

The purpose of professional training in group work is to prepare counselors, psychologists, and other mental health professionals to help people from a variety of racial and cultural groups to function better interpersonally and in groups and organizations. If we see groups as a microcosm of the larger society (Yalom, 1995), then a focus on issues such as race and culture in the training literature for group counseling and psychotherapy seems to be crucial in the preparation of mental health professionals. When people from different racial and cultural backgrounds come together, racial and cultural dynamics always exist and can become more salient than other dynamics. Racial and cultural dynamics can also mask other difficult dynamics such as competition, envy, and jealousy, which are common human characteristics in groups. The task for mental health professionals is to develop the competence to acknowledge and work with racial and cultural differences rather than ignore or deny their presence. If such differences are not addressed, clients will feel unheard and unseen in their humanity, and they may wonder if the mental health professional can truly understand the context and nature of their concerns. Moreover, clients may not fully trust that they will be accepted for who they are and for their unique contributions to the group experience.

Demographic transitions of the 21st century and the growing need for clinical group treatment in institutions serving diverse populations necessitates an understanding by mental health professionals of the influence of racial-cultural factors in interpersonal communication. Many books on group work have only one chapter on working with multicultural populations. Including multiple chapters on multiculturalism helps mental health professionals develop increased levels of multicultural competence. However, the authors of this text have found that race and culture are treated separately in many academic textbooks and thus not as an integral part of the counseling and psychotherapy process.

The purpose of this book is to offer a theoretical framework that embodies aspects of race and culture and an understanding of the covert and overt processes in group and organizational life. We use psychoanalytic (interpersonal and relational) and systems theory, examining the whole group and the conscious and unconscious processes that occur as they relate to racial and cultural issues. Conceptually, the model offered focuses on the group-as-whole rather than the individual. The premise is that the individual acts on behalf of the group, given the group norms and culture. Within each group or system, there are boundaries, authority issues, roles, and tasks to be considered that will vary according to the culture of the group, the members of the group, and the larger environment in which the group exists. The authors draw from a conceptual framework called group relations theory, which focuses on the group-as-a-whole. We integrate best practices in working with groups where the members have different racial and cultural backgrounds. Finally, racial-cultural differences often present challenges in a variety of environments—academic, clinical, not-for-profits, and for-profit organizations. Unrecognized and unprocessed racial and cultural dynamics can impede productive functioning in group and organizational life. This book addresses ways of recognizing, understanding, and managing these challenges. Throughout the book, we use the terms *racial-cultural groups* and *diverse groups* interchangeably to refer to the broad multicultural spectrum of people from all groups. Race, which has no "consensual biological or physiological definition" (Helms & Cook, 1999, as cited in D'Andrea & Daniels, 2001, p. 291), is commonly defined by physical characteristics related to skin color, hair texture, and facial features. Categorizations of race are based on socially constructed attitudes and beliefs that have their origins in positive and negative stereotypes related to access to power, privilege, and hierarchical levels of superiority and inferiority within society (D'Andrea & Daniels, 2001). Culture is defined as groups of people who share a common history, geographic region, language, rituals, beliefs, values, rules, and laws (Goldberger & Veroff, 1995). A contemporary definition of culture within a pluralistic society marks individuals with shared characteristics as members of a group. Thus, groups identified by race, gender, class, ethnicity, sexual orientation, disability, and age may call themselves "cultures," and be regarded as such by others, despite their membership in the larger culture and dissimilarities of histories, language, rules, beliefs, and cultural practices.

Throughout this book, we use our combined 30-plus years of experience teaching group dynamics, working with groups in a variety of settings, and our extensive training in conducting group relations conferences both nationally and internationally to illustrate our perspective. In the past few years, the first author (M.B.M.) has videotaped small study groups during weekend group relations conferences that were held at a large university in the northeast. We use examples from these groups to demonstrate many of the racial-cultural dynamics that we have seen in groups that we have worked with over the years. We integrate examples from group relations conferences with ones drawn from teaching and other observations and experiences that we have had during our years of working with groups. We have developed some examples from our different experiences in groups, and we have edited the examples from transcripts to make the conceptual points more clearly. Thus, the transcripts are used more for educational than for research purposes.

Group Relations Conferences

Group relations conferences are temporary educational laboratories constructed for the purpose of studying group and systemic behaviors as they occur in the "here and now" of the experience. There are a number of experiential events that take place during the course of the weekend or the longer residential (5–14 days) conference. Although the term *workshop* is probably more appropriate, the term *group relations conference* is used nationally and internationally for both short weekend and longer residential temporary educational laboratories or institutions. The conference opens with a plenary session to introduce the staff, the primary task, and the goals, events, and parameters of the experience. During the course of the conference, there are small and large study groups with consultants that meet approximately four times during the weekend and daily in other instances. There is an Intergroup Event, designed to examine the representation and relatedness of groups formed by participants; a plenary session to discuss the Intergroup Event; review and application groups to help participants integrate their learning with their external worlds; and a conference discussion to review their overall learning and experience of the entire conference. After the conference, follow-up sessions are held, sometimes to help members process and integrate their experiences and apply their learning to their personal and professional environments.

The examples presented in this book are from three conferences, all focusing on authority, leadership, and working with differences. The conferences had themes that focused on the exploration of racial and cultural differences as they related to authority, leadership, and transformation in group and organizational life. In the first conference, which was directed by the first author, there were seven small study groups that were configured with members from similar and diverse racial-cultural backgrounds. An African American man, who openly identifies as gay, directed the second conference (with the first author in the role of associate director). At this conference, one of six small study groups agreed to be videotaped for each of the four sessions held during the weekend. An African American woman directed the third conference. The second author (E.L.S.) of this text served as a consultant in all three conferences. Participants of the conferences were informed in the brochure for the conference that there would be a research or educational component to the conference that involved videotaping of the experience. Each person signed a consent form before participating. In the first conference, there were 83 participants, who were placed in seven groups, with 11 to 12 members. The conference director and the associate director assigned participants to small study groups according to how they self-identified in terms of color and culture. In the second and third conferences, one small study group was videotaped for each of the four sessions held during the weekend. There were 10 to 12 members in each of the small study groups.

In the first conference, there was one group with all people of color, one group with half Latina/o members, another one with members half of whom were gay or lesbian, one with all white members, one with predominantly white members, one with Middle Eastern and European members, and, finally, one group, which was labeled a "rainbow mix," with members from a variety of backgrounds. In this conference, each group was assigned a consultant with color and culture similar to half or the majority of members in the group. Therefore, African American women consulted to the people-of-color and the rainbow groups, a Latino man consulted to the half-Latina/o group, a gay man to the half-gay/lesbian group, a woman who was half Middle Eastern to the Middle Eastern/European group, a white man to the all-white group, and a white woman to the predominantly white group.

In the second conference, there were 81 members in all. The small group studied consisted of two white men (one who identified as Jewish and heterosexual, the other as homosexual), two black men (one heterosexual, the other gay), one Latino man (gay), and five white women (one member identified as German, one Catholic; all identified as heterosexual). The videotapes were transcribed by a professional transcription service. The authors read the transcripts and identified segments to be used as examples for certain racial-cultural group dynamics. In some cases, the authors have edited the transcripts so that the statements are more understandable for the purpose of making a conceptual point in the text.

Organization of the Book

We have organized this book into 10 chapters. Chapter 1 provides an overview of groups as psychodynamic systems in the context of racial-cultural factors.

Group work, via theories, application, and practice, has often failed to integrate racial-cultural factors. Our goal is to integrate multicultural concepts and traditional group relations theory. The exploration of racial-cultural factors in groups may be both parallel to and interactive with the processes of group dynamics (e.g., group norms, group membership and leadership, communication patterns, authority, power, dependency, interdependency, splitting, projection, and projective identification). The group relations approach to understanding groups seems particularly appropriate for the study of racial-cultural factors in groups. For example, in groups, the condition of invisibility, as it relates to racial-cultural dynamics, perpetuates the emergence of an "other" against which members and/or groups can differentiate and/or compare via the use of racist stereotypes and projections. The existence of the invisible other is currently, and has historically been, quite pervasive in a variety of professional environments, including academia. With regard to the academy, we hypothesize that an academic institution's inability to fully explore and embrace issues of race and culture within curricula, and particularly in group counseling and psychotherapy training programs, may be an example of reinforcing long held patterns of denial of the pervasiveness of these dynamics. Moreover, the hierarchical composition within these environments can represent the power differentials that exist in society. Despite the existence of these conditions, however, academic and training institutions are often reluctant to assess their internal racial and cultural climates. A reluctance to explore and discuss racial-cultural factors can lead to the development of curricula and training models that are etic and ethnocentric in content (Highlen, 1994). In light of the rapidly changing demographics in client/patient care, the perpetuation of curricula that ignore the importance of racial-cultural factors is not only harmful to emerging professionals, it is also unethical.

In Chapter 2, we focus on the ethical considerations of working with differences in groups. Competencies for group and organizational consultation developed by the A. K. Rice Institute for the Study of Social Systems (AKRI, 2003) are used as a framework to discuss the development of competent group practitioners. Guidelines for ethical behavior from multiple organizations, including the American Psychological Association (APA, 1993, 2002) and the American Counseling Association (ACA, 1995), are reviewed. Ethical issues concerning the use of experiential methods in group training are addressed, as well as a review of the importance of role clarity, leadership values, dual relationships, and informed consent. Ethical behavior related to racial-cultural dynamics in groups and the importance of developing competencies that include awareness, knowledge, and skills in working across differences are examined. Issues of confidentiality, supervision, and training are also discussed.

Chapter 3 focuses on the racial-cultural dynamics that affect group formation, specifically aspects of entering and joining. The chapter provides a basic understanding of the concept of group formation, focusing on boundaries, paradoxes of belonging, and the meaning of group membership, cognitively and emotionally, for members from different racial-cultural groups.

Chapter 4 explores the phases of group development and how racial-cultural factors affect a group's development. A brief review of the models of group development is provided as a way of understanding the anticipated events and patterns in which groups develop. The chapter outlines three phases of group development—boundaries, power, and relationships—and discusses how racial-cultural dynamics affect each phase. A review of the limited literature on group development of racially mixed groups is provided, as well as examples of some of the underlying issues that emerge in racially and culturally diverse groups during the phases of the group's life.

Chapter 5 explores the racial-cultural aspects of group dynamics, using psychoanalytic and systems theory as a foundation. The chapter outlines the defense mechanisms of splitting, projection, and projective identification. Group-as-a-whole (Wells, 1985, 1990) and embedded intergroup relations (Alderfer, 1997; Alderfer & David, 1988) theories are also outlined and explored as they relate to group functioning. Five types of basic assumption functioning (Bion, 1975; Hayden & Molenkamp, 2004) are defined and applied to group behavior. In this chapter, the authors also expand on existing theories and incorporate the racial-cultural factors that play an important role in group interactions, using case vignettes and tables to illustrate their perspective.

An examination of social roles in groups is the content of Chapter 6 and focuses on understanding the social roles in groups, specifically as they relate to phases of group development and racial-cultural factors. There is also a focus on the significance of social roles as they relate to group-as-a-whole, such as Leader, Follower, Mediator, Rebel, and Scapegoat. The impact of social roles in international contexts is examined.

Chapter 7 explores and defines authority, leadership, and power in groups. In many groups and organizations, the race and culture of individuals affect perceptions about their capacity to take up the role of leadership, the ways in which they are authorized in the role, and the power available to fully take up leadership. The impact of the internalized and the external messages pertaining to race and cultural values are examined.

In Chapter 8, strategies for working with groups are discussed using the AKRI training competencies as a framework for group work in a variety of types of groups. The chapter discusses the importance of assessing the needs of the group and the members' awareness and understanding of racial-cultural issues that may surface during all developmental stages of the group.

The mature work group is discussed in Chapter 9. The chapter focuses on the coexistence of the mature work group with the basic assumption group, making the point that a group that functions effectively is one that has learned to contain its anxiety or developed ways to mobilize its anxiety in the service of the group's goal or work task. Examples are provided to illuminate aspects of the mature work group when members are from different racial and cultural backgrounds. Finally, Chapter 10 explores the complexities of termination in groups. An application of cultural factors concerning the ending of groups is examined.

The lack of an abundant body of literature and research concerning race and culture in group work for training of mental health professionals is disturbing and unfortunate. The situation can, however, be viewed as an opportunity to expand on existing theories and create new models for the future. The goal of our book is twofold: (1) to offer a theoretical framework for understanding covert and overt processes in group and organizational life and (2) to present race and culture as integral parts of the counseling and psychotherapy process for mental health professionals who work with groups. If the profession of counseling and psychology is to continue serving society in meaningful ways, it is imperative that academic and other programs serving diverse populations develop and implement curricula, group counseling, psychotherapy training, and treatment programs that foster a perspective embodying a breadth of knowledge and sensitivity to the complexities of race, ethnicity, and culture in group life.

Acknowledgments

We would like to thank Robert Carter, who encouraged us to write this book; Leo Wilton and Zachary Green for their careful reviews and comments; and our many friends and colleagues who provided so much support during the time we were writing. We are also grateful to Sarah J. Brazaitis, Teachers College, Columbia University; Christopher J. McCarthy, University of Texas at Austin; James J. Messina, Argosy University, Tampa and Sarasota Campuses; and Brenda Frechette, Argosy University, San Francisco Bay Area, for reviewing this book.

1

Understanding Groups as Psychodynamic Systems in the Context of Racial and Cultural Factors

Theoretical Framework

The theoretical framework that we work from in this text can broadly be called *group relations theory*, as a model for working with groups. The model was developed at the Tavistock Institute for Human Relations in the United Kingdom, expanded on in conference settings by A. Kenneth Rice, and later brought to the United States by Margaret Rioch, who started the national organization called A. K. Rice Institute for the Study of Social Systems (Hayden & Molenkamp, 2004). The theoretical roots of the group relations model can be traced to Wilfred Bion (1961), Melanie Klein (1946), and Kurt Lewin (1951). There are two components in group relations theory, psychoanalytic and systems theory. Psychoanalytic theory helps us understand the conscious and unconscious processes that affect individual and group functioning. Psychoanalytic theory has been linked to race-cultural dynamics, specifically the phenomenon of racism, by a variety of theorists, including Dalal (2002), who has used the theories of Freud, Klein, Fairbairn, and Winnicott to examine racism. Earlier attempts to link psychoanalytic theory to racism have also been made by Fanon (1967) and Kovel (1984). In more recent years, self-psychology, relational theory, and positive psychology have been incorporated in the thinking of many psychoanalytically oriented psychologists such as Kohut (1980), Mitchell (1988), and Seligman (2002). The work on relational cultural theory by Jordan (2001) exploring the connections and disconnections in relationships has been particularly important to our work (McRae, Kwong, & Short, 2007).

1

Open Systems Theory and Experiential Learning

Applications of systems theory facilitate the understanding of the context in which a behavior occurs and the sociopolitical factors that may influence an individual's behavior. In this book, we use Alderfer's (1977) definition of a group, as follows:

> A collection of individuals 1) who have significantly interdependent relations with each other; 2) who perceive themselves as a group by reliably distinguishing members from non-members; 3) whose group identity is recognized by non-members; 4) who have differentiated roles in the group as a function of expectations from themselves, other members and non-group members; and 5) who as group members acting alone or in concert have significantly interdependent relations with other groups. (p. 230)

Groups, therefore, function as subsystems in larger systems, such as an organization, a community, a society, and the world. Thus, groups are embedded in larger groups and systems and in a social, economic, and political context.

Conceptually, the group relations model encompasses open systems and psychoanalytic theory to explore its premise that the individual acts on behalf of the group, given the group norms and the cultural context in which the group exists. "Within each group or system, there are boundaries, authority issues, roles, and tasks (BART) to be considered that will vary according to the culture of the group" (Green & Molenkamp, 2005; Hayden & Molenkamp, 2004). The concept of BART (boundaries, authority, roles, and tasks) is derived from open systems theory, which focuses on group boundaries, which are observable and subjective measures used to distinguish group members from outsiders. Boundaries in groups can be physical (observable) or psychological (subjective). Group boundaries can also be permeable or impenetrable, enmeshed or disengaged (McCollom, 1990). Management of group boundaries within systems encompasses aspects of time, space, task, territory, and role. Authority, which is the second aspect of BART, is defined as a group's right to perform tasks, use resources, and make decisions that may be binding on others (Obholzer, 1994). Authority can occur (a) from above (e.g., within organizational hierarchies); (b) from below, when given formally or informally by peers; and (c) from within, which refers to individuals' capacity to take up their own authority, to behave in certain ways within the group, based on their personality, their personal and racial-cultural history, and representations of authority within their own mind. Role, the third aspect of BART, refers to an individual's position or function in relation to the formal task and his or her own personal characteristics, which creates a valence for enacting certain behaviors. Finally, task in open systems theory is related to the primary task that the group needs to perform to survive. The group's task may be defined in multiple ways within the system and may therefore be implemented, impeded, avoided, and/or rebelled against by the group-as-a-whole.

There are five levels at which the group functions during its life: intrapersonal, interpersonal, group (group-as-a-whole), intergroup, and interorganizational (Wells, 1990). It is important, systemically, to consider the individual's personality characteristics, interpersonal relations and intergroup relationships between subgroups, and group-as-a-whole dynamics. Kurt Lewin's (1951) work on field theory and the notion of psychosociological influences over group behavior lead to a focus on examining the group-as-a-whole in a social context (Fraher, 2004). In addition, Lewin's discovery in 1946 that adults learn more effectively through interactive experiences shared in experiential learning environments (Fraher, 2004) has had a profound effect on how group relations theory is used in the field. Practitioners, educators, and group workers who use group relations theory often use experiential learning activities that help students and participants understand theory and concepts. Application of the group relations theory to didactic and experiential learning helps students and participants gain insight into the complex defense mechanisms of splitting, projection, and projective identification. Moreover, these concepts can be experienced in the "here and now" of the experiential setting and discussed, which enhances learning and application of theory.

Group Relations Theory

From a psychoanalytic perspective, groups engage in unconscious and conscious behaviors that are attributed to the anxiety that most people experience in groups and organizations. Using Klein's (1946) object relations theory, Bion (1961) noted that groups trigger primitive fantasies, such as the infantile desire to join others in an undifferentiated entity, while simultaneously creating fears of being rejected or abandoned by the group or of losing one's identity and sense of self. The tension between wanting to join the group and be independent from it often generates anxiety in its members and can lead them to defend against this anxiety through the mechanisms of splitting, projection, and projective identification. These defenses are unconscious processes and will be explained in more detail in later chapters. It is important to note that these unconscious processes distort reality, impede optimal functioning, and promote behaviors that can create a variety of both negative and positive feelings among group members. Bion (1961) hypothesized that groups had two modes of functioning: work and basic assumption. The work group attends to its primary task of group survival. Basic assumption group functioning represents an unconscious mode of group behavior that is focused on management of anxiety that surfaces related to the group's work. Thus, when the group members are engaging in basic assumption behavior, they are no longer attending to the primary focus of their task at hand. Originally, there were three basic assumption modes: dependency, fight-flight, and pairing, all of which serve as unconscious defense mechanisms against the anxiety created by the group in the service of accomplishing its primary task. A fourth mode, basic assumption oneness, was developed by Turquet (1985); the fifth basic assumption, or basic assumption me-ness, was developed by Lawrence, Bain, and Gould (1996). Both of these modes are also unconsciously used by group members to defend against anxiety created by their experience in the group. From a positive-psychology perspective, basic assumptions can be viewed as a way of managing anxiety. In groups, we look for ways of containing and channeling those emotions in a more productive manner.

Group relations as a theoretical model focuses on factors that have proven most successful in group counseling and psychotherapy training programs: didactic, observation, and experiential learning. The didactic component includes lectures about theory, as well as a collective sharing of reactions to readings and lectures about theory. Observations provide an opportunity to see and hear how others manage the role of consultant, leader, and facilitator, as well as client member. The experiential component allows for reflection on the here-and-now experience, as well as an understanding of the relationship between theoretical and experiential learning and the application of what has been learned. The experiential component also provides an opportunity to learn about aspects of anxiety as it relates to group membership in the here and now, for example, the tension caused by fears of identity fragmentation and engulfment by the group. While the current focus of the group relations model is on experiential learning, earlier conceptualizations of the model included a didactic component. In our group dynamics classes, we have found that readings, lectures, and discussions further enhance students' understanding and application of group dynamics.

From a systems perspective, groups are confronted with racial-cultural issues that are related to the power differentials, authority, and class hierarchies that exist in society. Thus, racial-cultural dynamics are phenomena that are an integral part of the group experience. Demographic variables such as race, ethnicity, culture, class, sexual identity, gender, disability, and age often represent differences between group members that may evoke negative stereotypes and stimulate feelings about inclusion and exclusion (McRae & Short, 2005). Differences that are visible or invisible may foster conflicts characterized by inclusion or exclusion; differences may also serve as a catalyst for feelings about membership to emerge. Membership may be affected by stereotyped assumptions about difference, which may influence group members' perceptions of themselves and the group-as-a-whole. For example, members who belong to the dominant racial-cultural group may perceive themselves or be perceived as powerful and privileged. Likewise, members who externally represent non-dominant groups may have self-perceptions of having less or more power given the particular context of the group (McRae & Short, 2005). Using systems theory allows a more direct examination of the intersection between racial-cultural factors and systemic factors such as power, authority, leadership, boundaries, roles, task, and interpersonal relations in the group experience.

From a psychoanalytic perspective, group processes involve paying attention to what occurs in the here-and-now experience of the group. Frequently, unconscious processes can occur that polarize racial-cultural groups. This polarity can be indicative of defense mechanisms, such as resistance, intellectualization, splitting, projection, and projective identification (Fenster, 1996). Group members may use intellectualization as a defense by the majority to focus on superficial cultural or racial attributes of those members in the minority (Fenster, 1996). Splitting and projective identification, while adaptive defenses in group life, can also be characterized, when used in diverse racial-cultural groups, as major defenses that are used to protect members against feelings of inadequacy and vulnerability (Cheng, Chase, & Gunn, 1998). One of the tasks of the group is to help make the unconscious conscious by speaking authentically to behaviors that occur in the group and attending to the nuances of speech and language and the nonverbal behaviors of members. When this type of processing can be done with racial-cultural group issues, it provides invaluable opportunities for learning. For example, many students who attend predominantly white institutions throughout their academic lives may never have had an African American professor. According to bell hooks (2003), in predominately white institutions, African American professors, particularly those who are female, may have their authority challenged by white students, who may not have had any relations with black people and thus may never have been in situations in which they have had to listen to a black person or a black woman speak to them for any length of time.

From a systems perspective, being a professor is a role with the authority to determine course content, method of teaching, and grading. If students are encountering an African American professor for the first time, what is the experience of these students? In our experience as African American female professors, students have questioned us in subtle and not so subtle ways about our credentials and work experience. It has become clear to us that in addition to the more traditional aspects of the role, being an academic professor also encompasses taking a role that is perceived by the students as incongruent for someone of our race and gender. Thus, a key question is "What are their perceptions of us in terms of personal characteristics such as race, gender, and our professorial role of authority and leadership?" The question then becomes

"Do students from diverse backgrounds feel that they will be treated fairly by a professor of color, and, moreover, why is this even a question for consideration?"

Distrust of a black professor does not exist only in white students. Depending on their level of racial identity development, some black students may perceive a black professor as too black identified or not black identified enough, based on their own identification with this racial reference group. For example, one of the coauthors' (M.B.M.) students, who is biracial and has a white mother, wondered if she could be accepted by the coauthor as the loving daughter of a white woman who had been treated badly by some black women who are adamantly against interracial marriages. Another example of this phenomenon in a larger, societal context is the critique that was leveled against President Obama, when he was a nominee and presidential candidate of the Democratic Party, by some members of the black communities in the United States as not being "black enough." This critique was based, in part, on his biracial and multicultural identities, as well as his political stance on issues of race. The election of President Obama created more opportunities to explore the complexities of authority and leadership in role as they relate to race and gender at the societal level.

Since racial-cultural factors in many societies encompass aspects of power, authority, and class or status hierarchies, the lack of attention to them prohibits exploration of a lived reality for many individuals. The lack of discussion concerning the existence of racial-cultural hierarchical dynamics may be reflective of existing societal structures that perpetuate the invisibility and institutionalization of a dominant culture in which privileges are readily available to some subgroups and not to others (McRae & Short, 2005). In a larger social-historical context, this ambivalence about exploring race and culture also has its roots in the American cultural experience. Toni Morrison (1992) in *Playing in the Dark: Whiteness and the Literary Imagination* postulates that silence and evasion about race have historically been viewed as effective methods of enforcing the invisibility of the African American presence within the dominant culture. This condition of invisibility perpetuates the emergence of an "other" with which one group can compare itself via the use of racist stereotypes and projections. While Morrison's focus is on African Americans, the "other" can easily be any disenfranchised group. We hypothesize, therefore, that the inability to fully explore and embrace issues of race and culture may be an example of reinforcing long held patterns of denial of the pervasiveness of racial-cultural dynamics within institutionalized environments.

Understanding the confluence of stereotypes, projection, and interpersonal style that exists within groups increases our ability to negotiate and collaborate among and between racial-cultural groups in society. In our work as professors and organizational consultants, we have used the group relations model to address the power hierarchies that we have encountered, in order to provide a foundation for the examination of systemic structures and their relationships to racial-cultural factors.

Research on Racial and Cultural Group Dynamics

There is a dearth of research on racial-cultural group dynamics. Most of the literature is in the form of anecdotal reports and case studies. Some of the research on intergroup relations has highlighted the complexity of racial-cultural group dynamics (Shaw & Barret-Power, 1998). McRae (1994) applied Helms's (1990) model of racial identity development to group dynamics using a case example of a study group of students of diverse races and genders (e.g., black and white, male and female) from a graduate class on group counseling. McRae (1994) concluded that racial identity attitudes are dynamic and dichotomous categorization of group members along racial lines concerning expected alliances and interactions may foster stereotypes and deemphasize the complexity of interracial group behavior.

Research that has been conducted on group formation and intergroup relations has also focused on stress, anxiety, and threat. These variables have been hypothesized to be the foundation of negative and/or uncomfortable intergroup encounters among individuals of diverse racial-cultural backgrounds. Mendes, Blascovich, Lickel, and Hunter (2002) examined the extent to which minority or "devalued" group members engendered threat reactions from interaction partners (p. 939). The researchers measured cardiovascular responses marking challenge and threat among participants (e.g., white, Asian, Latino, and Other) involved in social interactions with black or white male "confederates," who, during the experiment, described their socioeconomic backgrounds as either advantaged or disadvantaged (p. 939). Intergroup interactions in the study were hypothesized to result in perceived danger related to social dominance, cultural inferiority, increased effort to self-monitor, increased vigilance to verbal and nonverbal communication, and unconscious processes. Thus, the interactions with minority or "devalued" group members would involve greater perceived demands and/or fewer perceived resources than interactions with majority group members. The study's findings support the researchers' hypothesis that participants experience threat during social encounters with devalued group members; cardiovascular responses among participants interacting with black/disadvantaged socioeconomic status (SES) confederates were consistent with threat, and participants who interacted with white/advantaged SES confederates exhibited "significantly different" cardiovascular responses consistent with challenge responses (p. 950).

The impact of cultural diversity on work groups has also been researched. Thomas (1999) conducted a study examining the influence of cultural diversity on work groups, using collectivism (e.g., as in collectivist vs. individualist cultural attitudes) as the dimension of cultural variation for the study. The study's results supported previous research study findings that group-level assessments of cultural diversity, sociocultural norms of group members, and degrees of members' relative cultural distance from the group (e.g., as related to their attitudes about collectivism) were all factors influencing group effectiveness. Thus, the study's results suggested that understanding the dynamics of multicultural work groups is related not only to the group's level of cultural heterogeneity or homogeneity but also to the recognition that culturally different individuals often bring preconceived notions about work group functioning to the groups that they join (Thomas, 1999).

Other studies concerning racial-cultural dynamics of group formation and intergroup relations have also focused on aspects of threat, trust, and distrust as these variables relate to the projection of racist stereotypes (Govorun, Fuegen, & Payne, 2006) and perceived threat in social interactions with stigmatized others (Blascovich, Mendes, Hunter, Lickel, & Kowai-Bell, 2001). Greene (1999) also conducted a study on representations of group-as-a-whole, as related to personality, situation, and dynamic determinants among a group of participants at a group relations conference.

Stereotype threat is a phenomenon, defined by Steele and Aronson (as cited in Suzuki, Prevost, & Short, 2008), that occurs when the salience of race adversely affects the test-taking performance of high-ability African American students, specifically as it relates to anxiety that may be experienced based on stereotypes about an individual's racial and ethnic group affiliation. Another investigation of the impact of stereotype threat on black-white test score differences, by Sackett, Hardison, and Cullen (as cited in Suzuki et al., 2008), found that the impact of stereotype threat is an important phenomenon "because it highlights the fact that test scores can be influenced by factors other than the test takers' true level of skill and achievement" (Suzuki et al., 2008, p. 515). Thus, racial-cultural dynamics related to stereotypes have been found to have an impact on test-taking environments, classrooms, and other academic settings and have implications on group behaviors and performance outcomes in these settings. Moreover, the impact of stereotype threat is applicable to a variety of group settings outside the academy—for instance, mental health environments.

The complex effects of race, ethnicity, and diversity related to racial-cultural factors of group and intergroup relations at the societal and community levels have also been focused on in the print media. An article by Erica Goode in the *New York Times Magazine* (2007) posited that increased diversity within communities, instead of fostering tolerance and trust, can engender a desire for individuals to "stick to their own groups and distrust those who are different from them," thus resulting in a state of isolation (p. 24). Goode then suggests that diverse community initiatives will require a certain amount of time before individuals become comfortable. On a more positive note, the article points to the rising rates of interracial marriage among the younger generation, resulting in changing attitudes about diversity, as a marker of how racial and ethnic differences can become less salient at the societal level.

In a larger societal context, the 2008 presidential election surfaced long suppressed issues regarding the complexity of race and culture in the United States. For example, during the primaries, one of the most frequently discussed debates concerned the struggle of individuals and the media to manage anxieties about the salience of race versus gender as they related to Senators Hillary Clinton (a white woman) and Barack Obama (a black, biracial man) as candidates of the Democratic Party. The election of Senator Obama as the Democratic Party's presidential candidate further highlighted a racial-cultural dialogue about the historical significance of his candidacy, as well as the real and symbolic meaning of what having an African American man as president would mean for race relations in the United States and internationally. Some of the dialogues about Obama's suitability for the office of president engendered a subtle, underlying focus regarding race that questioned his ability or readiness to lead, his level of experience, and the quality of his judgment. These are commonly used qualifiers that may label an applicant or candidate of African descent as less qualified to take up leadership roles. Additional research on racial-cultural group dynamics within the United States and internationally will be included in subsequent chapters of this text.

Application and Universality of the Group Relations Model

As with psychoanalytic theory, the group relations model was developed by white Europeans in the United Kingdom and thus complements the traditions of a Eurocentric society. However, we have found that it is a model with widespread applications across race and culture. Our rationale for the expanded application of the model is related to a conclusion drawn by Slavson in 1956 that fundamentally the psychological needs, anxieties, and motivations of individuals are more similar than different. Thus, historical and cultural patterns may cause individuals to behave differently, but they may be united in their emotional responses to a variety of stimuli at the group level. Slavson suggested and Yalom (1995) stated that certain curative factors in groups, such as instillation of hope, universality or knowing that one is not alone in what one is feeling, catharsis (expression of emotions), altruism, reenactment of family dynamics for corrective experiences, and interpersonal learning, are constant across differences.

We believe that the group relations model provides a mechanism for learning and experiencing emotions and understanding them in the context of the group. Knowledge about group dynamics can also be applied to systemic, organizational, and societal functioning. In this book, we use this conceptual frame as a mechanism for understanding the role of the individual in the context of the group-as-a-whole and tasks of the group or institution and for understanding the psychodynamic processes that occur within and between various social identity groups. Behaviors in groups and organizations are open to observation and analysis by all those who participate, if they care to see and reflect. We have adapted the group relations model for teaching group dynamics and helping students develop competencies that will facilitate increased self- and group awareness of racial-cultural factors as they relate to systemic and organizational processes. Our goal is to provide opportunities to learn through experience and reflection, using both intellect and emotions, thus allowing students to explore, model, and discuss behavioral group dynamics. We use a combination of theoretical concepts and experiential work to explore interactions in the here and now as they occur. Thus, cognitions, behaviors, and emotions can be identified and explored simultaneously. We believe, therefore, that a psychodynamic and systemic approach to understanding groups will significantly enhance students' learning and training in counseling and psychology.

Summary

In this chapter, we have presented an overview of the conceptual framework for the book. The group relations model, which is a combination of psychoanalytic and systems theory, was presented as the theoretical framework for examining racial and cultural dynamics in groups throughout this text. This approach allows an exploration of group dynamics in the context of the larger environment. It takes into consideration the conscious and unconscious processes that influence the interactions of members who belong to diverse racial-cultural groups. The rather scant research on racial-cultural dynamics in groups was addressed. Finally, we discussed the expanded application of the group relations model to incorporate, analyze, and assess racial-cultural group dynamics. In this chapter, we have laid the foundation from which we analyze groups; it is one lens from which to view group dynamics and the racial and cultural dynamics that we believe exist in every group.

QUESTIONS FOR REVIEW AND DISCUSSION

1. What are the theoretical roots of the group relations model?

2. Describe the BART concept, and apply it to a situation or system you are familiar with.

3. What psychoanalytic concepts are the most relevant in the group relations model, and how can they be helpful in understanding racial-cultural group dynamics?

4. What can institutional ambivalence about exploring race and culture be linked to in the larger social-historical context of the American cultural experience?

KEY TERMS AND CONCEPTS

BART   Group relations model

Culture   Racial-cultural groups

Defense mechanisms

2

Working With Differences in Groups

Ethical Considerations

A Chinese student who is in her first semester in a mental health graduate program at a large university in the United States speaks English with difficulty. She volunteers to participate in a fishbowl group in a group dynamics class. The task of the fishbowl group is to practice group work skills. In her member role, she talks about her difficulty adjusting to living in a new country. Due to her challenges with the English language, the professor and group members find her comments very difficult to understand. However, despite their difficulty in understanding the student, the professor, the student who is taking up the leader role, and the other group members do not ask for clarification from the student, nor do they inform her of their difficulty in understanding what she says. On the contrary, they nod their heads and smile as if they understand what she has said. The group continues as if everyone understands the Chinese student's comments.

In a world of racial and cultural differences, it is important to embrace professional standards for competence and training, especially if we expect to engage individuals from diverse backgrounds in group work. Professional principles and standards help create an environment of respect and integrity for individual and group differences. In the vignette above, the question of whether the professor needs to address the group members' behavior of acting as if they understood the Chinese student, and the ethical implications of allowing people to think that they are understood when they are not, is an important one in today's multicultural environment. The students in the fishbowl may feel uncomfortable at the prospect of stating that they do not understand what their peer is saying. The students may also feel awkward because they do not speak or comprehend the Chinese student's language of origin. Moreover, they may feel impatient with the situation and may not want to take the time to have the Chinese student repeat herself, which would serve to create an environment in which all members are working together in an effort to understand each other. The Chinese student may also feel uncomfortable and anxious about her level of fluency in English. She may also have a desire to express herself in her language of origin, and she may feel inhibited from acknowledging her feelings openly. Ethically, what does this mean for the clinical training of the Chinese student as well as the others in the class? What message is being sent to the students about the importance of engaging in authentic dialogue? In this instance, the issue of doing no harm and attending to the welfare of the student in training needs to be addressed by the professor.

Multiculturalism and Ethical Guidelines

Many people from groups that have experienced marginalization and disenfranchisement are skeptical about mental health and social service providers. Sue and Sue (2008) state that clients who do not speak Standard English, have pronounced accents, or have limited fluency in English may be victimized in therapeutic environments. The group setting presented in the vignette, while not therapeutic, embraces a training model that is culture-bound, stressing the importance of a focus on self-disclosure and verbal, emotional, and behavioral expressiveness. In this case, although the Chinese student is not a client, she is, as a student in training, being marginalized by the groups' withholding information about their difficulty in understanding what she is saying, by their not being honest with her, and by their failing to help her become more aware that others outside the group may have similar challenges in understanding her (especially her potential clients, who may not speak her language). This is an incident that could easily be generalized to therapeutic group settings with international clients. The influences of immigration, acculturation, and assimilation are important to consider in this context. For example, there is a growing population of Asians, as well as of individuals from other racial and ethnic groups whose ancestors emigrated to the United States either years ago or more recently. Some of these individuals have assimilated into American culture, having both American and bicultural identities, and thus may not experience any challenges with language fluency. Others struggle with language and cultural issues.

The Office of Ethnic Minority Affairs of the American Psychological Association (APA, 1993) has published "Guidelines for Providers of Psychological

Services to Ethnic, Linguistic, and Culturally Diverse Populations," which recommends that psychologists recognize and respect ethnicity and culture as significant parameters in understanding cultural differences and psychological processes regarding family, language, community, religion, spirituality, and sociopolitical issues. The Association for Specialists in Group Work's (ASGW, 2000b; http://www.asgw.org) "Principles for Diversity: Competent Group Workers" states as follows:

> Issues of diversity affect group process and dynamics, group facilitation, training, and research. As an organization, we recognize that racism, classism, sexism, heterosexism, ableism, and so forth affect everyone. As individual members of this organization, it is our personal responsibility to address these issues through awareness, knowledge, and skills.

The multicultural and diversity guidelines and principles are essentially geared to promote awareness, knowledge, and skill and to limit cultural encapsulation of group workers (Sue, Arredondo, & McDavis, 1992). The term *group worker* is used by ASGW to capture the variety of ways the counseling professionals work with groups. Thus, the term is used to identify a broad group of professionals who engage in working with groups in a variety of ways that includes group counseling, group facilitation, group psychotherapy, and group consultation.

According to the "Principles for Diversity-Competent Group Workers" (ASGW, 2000b), group workers with multicultural competence have an awareness of their own attitudes and beliefs, knowledge about their own race, ethnicity, SES, gender, sexual orientation, abilities, religion, and spirituality and how these aspects of self might affect those they work with. They also seek to develop themselves through educational, consultative, and training experiences in order to help them better understand and work more effectively with groups different from their own. Group workers engage in developing an awareness of the worldviews of group members from different racial and cultural backgrounds, possess specific knowledge about the life experiences and social context of various social identity groups, and develop skills for facilitating groups across differences. Intervention strategies for working across differences include awareness and respect for religious and spiritual differences and valuing bilingualism and other languages, as opposed to viewing them as an impediment to group work. The principles also promote an understanding of social context and systems and how they affect peoples' lives, especially the hierarchies of social class and other forces that influence interpersonal and group behavior. The multicultural and diversity guidelines that have been adopted by the above organizations owe much to a group of multicultural psychologists who have worked very diligently in addressing the multicultural issues related to ethics (see Pedersen, 1995; Sue et al., 1992). Pedersen (1995) addressed some of the weaknesses of the ethical principles, such as their bias toward the individualistic perspective, the pull for minorities to adapt to majority cultural standards, and the assumption of "one size fits all" (p. 45).

The A. K. Rice Institute for the Study of Social Systems (AKRI), the organization that founded the group relations model in the United States, describes its mission and purpose as a national educational institution for the advancement of the study of social systems and group relations. It seeks to deepen the understanding and the analysis of complex systemic, psychodynamic, and covert processes that give rise to nonrational behavior in individuals, groups, organizations, communities, and nations (www.akriceinstitute.org). AKRI has implemented a set of competencies for consultants in group relations conferences that offer some guidelines appropriate for a broad spectrum of group work professionals. The first phase of competencies indicates whether a person has basic observational skills that serve as a foundation for group work: "(1) Demonstrates general curiosity about what is happening in the group-as-a-whole; (2) Demonstrates the capacity to accept the experiences of others to be as valid as his/her own; and (3) Demonstrates the ability to be reflective and self-examining" (AKRI, 2003). In the second phase of training, the trainee is expected to develop additional competencies that require more in-depth ability to examine unconscious processes and to demonstrate an ability for self-containment of one's own emotions so as to distinguish the difference between self, the group's emotional state, and that of the surrounding environment. Developing the competence to demonstrate a reflective ability to self-examine in role and to own mistakes in front of group members and staff associates is an important skill to acquire. Demonstrating this level of competence shows that an individual can take risks, make mistakes, and recover in a professional manner when working with diverse group members. Developing the capacity to recognize that each individual holds or expresses some aspect of the group-as-a-whole and that the group operates in the context of a broader societal level grounds events in the social, political, and economic context of experience and can be a crucial factor when working across differences.

In this chapter on ethics, we join Brabeck and Ting (2000) in calling for a mandate for creating fair and ethical structures in groups and organizations that ensure that all people are cared for attentively so as to nurture the potential of each group member. For those who are group workers with racially and culturally diverse groups, the issues of power in the context of the group and the broader society, levels of acculturation, and racial identity development can influence behavior that could unintentionally or intentionally do harm to members (Frame & Williams, 2005). Working with subtle and intense racial and cultural dynamics that can surface in multicultural groups can create some challenges to the personal morals and cultural values of the group worker, especially when the clients' worldviews are very different. Ethical codes outline expectations for professional behavior, and in most cases there can be serious consequences for not adhering to them. For example, licensed professionals can risk losing their license, while others could face expulsion from professional organizations. There are potential legal ramifications for inappropriate behavior as well. We live and work in an increasingly multicultural world, and it is crucial that group workers develop awareness, knowledge, and skill in working with members from different racial, ethnic, and cultural backgrounds. Due to the complexity of multiple factors in multicultural groups, competency in working with differences is a dynamic process that requires practice and openness to different worldviews and behaviors that at first may seem unfamiliar and very different to the group worker and, possibly, to other members in a group.

We also concur with Ridley, Liddle, Hill, and Li (2001), who state that the process of "making ethical decisions in multicultural counseling and therapy is a professional's multicultural responsibility" (p. 176). The authors define *multicultural responsibility* as a "fusion of personal and professional commitments to consider culture during all ethical encounters" (p. 176). They outline five criteria for the attainment of multicultural responsible ethical assessment and behavior for all mental health professionals: (1) examining one's philosophical assumptions about culture and ethics and making these assumptions explicit, by, for example, identifying racial stereotypes and biases within oneself and considering how these assumptions affect interactions with clients; (2) examining alternative philosophical assumptions that one may hold about culture and ethics, for example, becoming more knowledgeable about racial and feminist theories; (3) increasing one's understanding of the ways that culture is always relevant in counseling and therapy; maintenance of this view may help the practitioner to recognize the salience of cultural issues in the therapeutic relationship; (4) developing complex and creative thinking skills about multiculturalism and ethics, as opposed to more rigid or inflexible problem solving; and (5) making an emotional investment in multicultural responsibility that would take precedence over intellectual or professional investments.

Most professional organizations have established codes of ethics that are available on their Web sites. Those organizations most relevant to group workers doing counseling, psychotherapy, consultation, facilitation, coaching, teaching, and research are the APA, the American Counseling Association (ACA), the National Association of Social Workers (NASW), and the American Association for Marriage and Family Therapy (AAMFT). The ASGW, a division of ACA, developed a set of best-practice guidelines (ASGW, 2000a), in addition to their "Principles for Diversity: Competent Group Workers" (ASGW, 2000b), which provide critical information for practitioners and scientists.

Principles of Ethical Behavior

Ethical codes are based on moral principles of behavior that are geared to protect the welfare and rights of the client. There are five principles that provide
the foundation for the ethical codes: beneficence, nonmaleficence, autonomy,
justice, and fidelity (Kitchner, 1984; Welfel & Kitchner, 1999).

Beneficence refers to promoting the welfare of the individuals and of the
group-as-a-whole. Promoting the welfare of others requires some awareness
and knowledge about who the members of the group are. It also requires some
knowledge about the historical relatedness of the subgroups represented by
members and how the boundaries between these groups have been managed,
as well as some awareness about the effect of these experiences on the current
socioeconomic and political context of general life circumstances. Being aware
of the social context creates awareness of its impact on individuals and their
relatedness to others and allows the group worker to provide services for the
betterment of each member and the group-as-a-whole.

Nonmaleficence refers to avoiding situations that could potentially harm
others as well as doing no harm to others. When group members come from
diverse backgrounds, there is the potential for unintentional behaviors related
to attitudes and to beliefs and feelings about self, one's identity group, and
other members from different racial and cultural groups to impede group
processes. Recent work conducted by Sue et al. (2007) on *racial microaggressions*, a concept that describes "daily verbal, behavioral, or environmental
indignities, whether intentional or unintentional, that communicate hostile,
derogatory, or negative racial slights and insults toward people of color" (p. 273),
suggests that group workers who are not aware of potential biases inherent in
them and others in society may, along with members of the group, act as per-
petrators of microaggressive behavior toward people of color as well as those
from other stigmatized or disenfranchised groups.

Autonomy refers to being respectful of the right of others to make their
own decisions about life choices. For group workers, this means that we are
aware and respectful of the different forms of verbal and nonverbal expressions
of group members from different racial and cultural backgrounds. For example, lack of eye contact and silence in a group are not necessarily acts of avoidance and resistance or a power ploy to obtain attention. Members have a right
to make choices that are grounded in their own cultural traditions and that
may be very different for the group worker and other members. For instance,
some cultures view direct eye contact, particularly with those in positions
of authority, to be rude and/or inappropriate. Moreover, some cultures do not
value verbalizations as highly as, for example, American culture does. Emotional expressiveness, which is often the goal of individual and group counseling, may also be viewed as taboo in some cultures that value restraint of strong
feelings (Sue & Sue, 2008).

Justice or fairness refers to treating members fairly. It requires a balancing of member interests in a manner that is clearly defined. For group workers, this involves acknowledging the context of power and the reality of privilege in many different forms (e.g., white privilege, gender privilege, social class, ethnic, heterosexual, age, etc., given the social context of the group) and how they affect the work and behavior of the group.

Fidelity or "being faithful to commitments" and the capacity to be loyal to one's words and promises create trustworthiness in the group worker's relationship with group members (Welfel & Kitchner, 1999, p. 135). Group members from different social identity groups often scrutinize the leader for signs of credibility. Credibility is related to how the role is taken up in terms of authority, consistency of behavior, identity, and SES (Sue & Sue, 2008). The skill of the group worker in demonstrating awareness of racial and cultural issues as well as knowledge about the historical relatedness of the groups represented by members will be observed and taken up quite seriously by members. Individuals from minority groups are usually very conscious of this but may not feel comfortable speaking about it in a group. The skill for group workers lies in the ability to hold on to the knowledge they acquire during the life of the group until they learn more about who the individual members are and how they may or may not be affected by their respective group identities. For example, a consultant in a small study group acknowledged the differences among members in a general sense but did not speak to any specific differences. The mention of the differences opened an avenue for a Jewish man in his 50s to speak to the tension he felt toward a young woman in the group who proudly claimed her German nationality. The young woman was surprised; the Holocaust and Germany's role in it was not something that had been talked about much in her family or community. She was more concerned about age than ethnic differences or historical relatedness between groups and individuals. In these types of group scenarios, the group worker's awareness, knowledge, and comfort level in working with differences helps create an environment that will enhance open, honest discussions and fidelity in the group.

Ethical Issues in Group Work

Some of the ethical issues most prominent in multicultural groups are training, role clarity and values of the leader, dual relationships, informed consent, and psychological risks to members.

TRAINING

Over the past 20 years, professional organizations such as ACA (1995) and APA (2002) have implemented guidelines specifically geared to develop multicultural competence among counselors and psychologists. One of the criticisms of the ethical codes is that they impose one set of behaviors of the dominant culture on all groups with no regard for diverse cultures (Pedersen, 1997). This focus on one set of behaviors can lead to cultural encapsulation where reality is defined in a one-dimensional perspective and the multiplicity of cultural values is ignored (Pedersen, 1997; Wrenn, 1985). Multicultural guidelines call for group workers to develop awareness and knowledge of their own racial, ethnic, and cultural selves as well as that of their client population and to demonstrate skill in working effectively with attitudes and stereotypes that might lead to discriminatory or biased behavior (Sue et al., 1992). These guidelines were an important step in recognizing the need for a multidimensional perspective when working with multicultural populations.

AKRI competencies for group relations consultants pay attention to the covert and unconscious aspects of behavior (Hayden & Carr, 1993). From a group relations perspective, the professional working competently with diverse groups is (1) curious about others; (2) has the ability to self-examine and to reflect on their own behavior as well as that of others; (3) is able to acknowledge his or her own mistakes publicly when necessary; (4) is aware of power differentials related to social identity factors that exist in groups, organizations, and the broader societal context; (5) is able to maintain a professional role and work within the boundaries of the stated task of the group when confronted with both positive and negative reactions from others; and (6) has an understanding and appreciation for the complexity and range of unconscious processes (AKRI, 2003).

When group members come from diverse backgrounds, there is the potential for unintentional biased behaviors related to attitudes, beliefs, and feelings to affect group dynamics. The group worker needs to be aware of their biases and open to confronting other possible biases that may be stimulated by group membership. Issues of oppressed versus oppressor or victim versus victimizer in the group can stimulate unresolved feelings in the group worker and make it difficult to work in a fair and just manner for the group-as-a-whole. It is the group worker's role to be aware of intergroup characteristics such as boundaries, power, affect, and belief systems that members hold about their own group and other groups and to be open to exploring these aspects within themselves before working with others.

Training for diversity-competent group workers requires both didactic and experiential learning formats. The authors of this text believe that creating experiential learning opportunities allows students and/or trainees to actually experience the application of theoretical concepts and to make conscious decisions about future practices in similar situations. Experiential learning also helps those in training to identify blind spots that could keep them culturally encapsulated. Internal exploration of the self in the group relations conceptual frame requires awareness of your racial ethnic identity attitudes, perceptions, and stereotypes about your own group and others. It also requires emotional exploration of unconscious feelings that affect behavior unintentionally. According to the AKRI Training Competencies (AKRI, 2003) there are three competencies that focus on internal work for the group consultant. First is the ability to work with unconscious processes in self and the group, and second is the ability for self-containment of emotions, to "hold still long enough" in order "to identify and feel along the boundary between what resides in the group and the environment and what resides in one's self" (p. 3). The third competency is the ability to examine one's professional role in a reflective manner in front of group members and the staff one is working with, while retaining or regaining one's professional role. Experiential learning can greatly enhance the development of these competencies for student trainees.

Competent group workers learn to track their own behaviors as well as the behaviors in the group, being mindful of who said what, when, and how; the pattern of verbal and nonverbal communication; the tone of the group; and what all of this has triggered for the individual group worker emotionally. Group workers monitor their own feelings as they work with the group. When conducting a group with members from different racial and cultural backgrounds, it is important to track events in terms of the specific identity groups while remembering that personality as well as racial-cultural factors are at play in the group. For example, the authors of this text come from working-class backgrounds. In working with people from middle- and upper-income backgrounds, our own social-class origins may trigger a multitude of feelings, including those of inadequacy regarding access to educational and economic resources. Continued self-exploration has helped us acknowledge the irrationality of these emotions, given the status of our present privileged positions as academics and organizational consultants; it has also helped us to be aware of how these dynamics could affect our work with the groups that we teach and/or consult to. When group workers are able to self-contain emotionally and to engage in self-examination, they increase their capacity to distinguish between the projected material of the group and their own projections that may be related to countertransference and/or unresolved issues that need to be worked on in personal therapy and/or professional supervision.

ROLE CLARITY AND LEADER VALUES

Clarity of roles and leader values help to create clear boundaries for engagement of the group. This is important, as "one's own identity and history affect one's work as well as calling forth particular fantasies and projections from others in a group context" (AKRI, 2003, p. 3). When group workers have an understanding of their own identity and history and what it might represent for those in the group, they can be more in touch with the emotional state of the group. Becoming aware of one's multiple identities, internalized messages about the social identity groups, and cultural values that one may hold will help individuals take up their professional roles more effectively. At times, group workers may need to acknowledge their own values in service of making the group members aware that one of the tasks of the group is to explore group members' values, attitudes, and belief systems for the group to make more informed choices (Corey & Corey, 2006).

The group worker's role and values may be influenced by the power attributed to their role by the group members and by their personal identity. Thus, the race, ethnicity, gender, age, sexual orientation, and religion (when obvious or when the information is provided) of the individual may influence how he or she takes up the role of group leader, especially in certain contexts. Some of the questions that group workers might ask themselves are "Is my role as facilitator or leader congruent with the group members' social identities?" and "How secure am I in taking up my work role, given my own social identity?" Lack of clarity or ambiguity of role and authority experienced by the group worker will be observed by the members, consciously and unconsciously, and will have an impact on the work of the group.

The perception of roles associated with class, race, and gender is a part of the socialization process for many individuals. Our perception of role is something that exists for both the group worker and the group member. Group workers are responsible for maintaining their role, which allows members to have an opportunity to try different roles. In doing this, the group worker provides a sense of consistent containment for the group. Different cultures attribute different values to role. Thus, in certain cultures, the role of the leader is perceived as the ultimate authority, someone who should not be challenged, while in Western cultures, challenging someone in authority is acceptable behavior. Age, gender, and social status, as they relate to authority, are also valued differently in various cultures.

Group workers should have some clarity about their own cultural values. The model presented by Kluckhohn and Strodtbeck (1961) is a useful framework for understanding individual and group differences. They provide four dimensions of human relations: time focus, human activity, social relations, and people/nature relationships. Different cultural values are associated with each of these dimensions. Thus, some cultural values are oriented to focusing more on the past, while others are more present or future oriented. Some cultures value human activity as just being or being and becoming, while others are more action oriented. In terms of social relations, some cultures value lineal or hierarchical relations, while others are more collectivist or individualistic. Perceptions of the leader role may vary according to members' cultural values. For example, members whose values are more lineal may feel more uncomfortable questioning the role of the group worker, and those from collectivist cultures may have a strong sense of duty inter-personally and may tend not to question role. It is therefore important for group workers to be aware of their value orientation regarding these dynamics and how their beliefs will influence their work with a diverse group of members. Pedersen (1997) suggests that a major concern is unwillingness on the part of mental health professionals to acknowledge that in most instances the majority cultural values are imposed on minority clients. The favoring of the dominant culture allows for cultural encapsulation of group workers and will limit their ability to empathize and understand the cultural values of group members from diverse backgrounds.

DUAL RELATIONSHIPS

Dual relationships refers to the importance of maintaining role and bound-ary between the group worker and the group members. Group workers are warned to avoid dual or overlapping roles, to separate personal and social roles from professional ones. Group workers have a fiduciary obligation to recognize group members' emotional vulnerability (Welfel, 2002). Members of a racial and culturally heterogeneous group may perceive the role of the group worker differently. The role of group worker is one that carries a status and power dif-ferent from that of group members. The group worker usually has the power to determine who stays in the group, sets the time and place of meetings, and provides and ensures the group a safe enough environment in which to work. If the group worker develops personal relationships with one or several group members outside the group, it could jeopardize the safety and trust needed for successful group work.

Another concern of dual relationships in academic settings is the require-ment for students to participate in experiential groups led by educators as a part of their course work. This is a situation that could involve a conflict of interest because students may feel vulnerable about their participation due to the authority of the professor to provide an evaluation and a course grade. This conflict can be resolved by (a) employing post-master's students to lead expe-riential groups, (b) using a blind-grading system, (c) requiring students to par-ticipate in external groups, or (d) using "fishbowl" training techniques, where students co-lead and the instructor observes and helps to process group dynamics (Gladding, 2003).

INFORMED CONSENT

Informed consent, according to the "Best Practices Guidelines" (ASGW, 2000a), involves providing information on the nature, purpose, and goals of the group; the services to be provided; the roles and responsibilities of leaders and group members; and the qualifications of the leaders to conduct the group. Those who participate in therapeutic and educational groups need to be well-informed so that they can make informed choices about their participation in the group. Since groups can be quite challenging emotionally, it is important that potential members have a clear idea of what is expected of them. Members need to be informed about the ambiguity and complexity of groups, since it is impossible to anticipate the course of the group's work (Lakin, 1999).

When working with individuals who are inexperienced or who have never done group work, it is important that they receive instruction in a respectable manner, in language that is appropriate to their level of understanding. It is important to inform prospective group members about what will happen and how they will know that they are improving and/or learning from the group experience, as well as the consequences of being absent or not participating.

PSYCHOLOGICAL RISKS

Learning about self in the context of a group can be exciting but challenging. Corey and Corey (2006) describe five potential psychological risks of therapeutic groups: self-disclosure, scapegoating, confrontation, maintaining confidentiality, and inadequate leadership. In this chapter, we have discussed these risks and modified them for working with racial and cultural differences. In diverse groups, vulnerability could be related to the power differential that exists between the group members and the historical relatedness of the various social identity groups represented, especially when these identities are salient to the experience of the members. Group members, whether they care to or not, can be perceived as representative of one or multiple social identity groups, with some being more salient than others, given the context of the group. Power differentials and histories of warring groups, ethnic cleansing, enslavement, the Holocaust, and religious conflicts can create tensions between group members and make it difficult to self-disclose. These types of challenges can lead to certain members being targeted as scapegoats within the group. Under these circumstances, confrontation can be more difficult or may be experienced in more threatening ways. Members may feel compelled to discuss their experiences outside the group with members of their own identity group so as to receive more support and empathy. These potential psychological risks require the group worker to be skilled in working with differences.

1. *Self-disclosure:* Self-disclosure is essential in groups because it creates a cohesive atmosphere where members can share personal information and learn that they are not alone with their feelings (Yalom, 1995). However, members should receive guidelines about appropriate types of self-disclosure and assistance in determining what to disclose and when self-disclosure is facilitative to the

group's process and development (Corey & Corey, 2006). Members of minority groups who have experienced discrimination and racism may be less open to self-disclosure in mixed-race groups. The continued experience of racial microaggressions, as described by Sue et al. (2007), may make it more difficult for individuals who may fear experiencing pain and disappointment. The group worker's awareness and sensitivity to group members' anxieties about the potential risks of self-disclosure in cultural contexts will allow them to work at creating a safe enough environment for all member self-disclosures.

2. *Scapegoat:* This is a form of destructive role differentiation in groups where one member is targeted as being the holder of negative and undesirable attributes. In a biblical sense, the scapegoat represents the sins of the tribe and must be sent into the wilderness for atonement (Wells, 1990). For example, in a small study group that consisted of about half black and half Asian members, two of the Asians were men (all the black members were women), one a young student, the other a mature mental health professional. During the group sessions, there was tension between the Asian and black women as they struggled for power and leadership in the group. The younger Asian man became the scapegoat in the group due to his behavior of saying things that the other members may have felt but were too embarrassed to say. For instance, he questioned whether the African American women could identify with Africa only as a continent, not as many countries with specific and diverse cultural values. In saying things that the others members found difficult to say, this member represented the bad parts, the competition and anger, of the other members. He seemed to willingly take up the role and then informed the group that he was aware that they were making him their scapegoat.

In racially mixed groups, the risk of those who belong to minority groups that are stigmatized due to race, social class, religion, sexual identity, or physical challenge is to become the target and/or the representative of otherness and negativity in the group. In another small study group, a Latina became the scapegoat in the group when she refused to participate verbally. The other members reacted negatively to her silence and eventually began to blame her for the group's difficulty in moving along. Her affect indicated that she seemed to enjoy the attention she received from the other members, and she continued to be silent in the small group. In the small study group, this woman seemed to hold the unspeakable, unmovable, angry parts for the group. However, during the large group sessions, a group setting that often seems more challenging for members to speak in, she spoke regularly. The scapegoat can be a necessary part of group development and member interaction. However, when behavior toward the individual who is being scapegoated is allowed to escalate, it can be dangerous to the survival of the group, primarily because it isolates the negative feelings in one member. It is the responsibility of the group worker to help the members identify scapegoating behavior, primarily by acknowledging that

it is occurring and identifying projective processes within the group that contribute to this type of behavior. The members need to have assistance in taking
back projections and freeing the member who is being scapegoated from
assuming full responsibility for the negative feelings and anxiety experienced
by the group (Wells, 1990).

3. *Confrontation:* Confrontation in groups is usually done with the goal of increasing awareness and initiating change (Kline, 2003). However, it is a powerful tool
that can elicit defensiveness, especially when it is done in a manner that is perceived as aggressive and/or hostile. The power differential and historical differences that serve as a backdrop for racial and culturally mixed groups require the
group worker to be unafraid to confront members who are from different social
identity groups. However, confrontation must be done with respect, awareness,
and an openness to explore how members may perceive the confrontation.

4. *Maintaining confidentiality:* Confidentiality refers to the right of group
members to discuss their feelings and thoughts in the group with the expectation that others will not disclose this information outside the group (Gladding,
2003). The psychological risk in racially and culturally mixed groups is the pull
to discuss fears and difficult experiences in the group with those of similar
backgrounds and values outside the group. It is the group worker's responsibility to inform members of the importance of confidentiality at the outset of
the group and to model this behavior as a way of setting a group norm (Corey
& Corey, 2006). While confidentiality is noted as one of the keystones for effective group work, ACA's *Code of Ethics and Standards of Practice* (1995), Section
B, states that group workers must inform group members that confidentiality
cannot be guaranteed. The group worker is also responsible for informing
group members of the consequences of not maintaining confidentiality, that it
is inappropriate, and that it is possibly hurtful to members.

5. *Inadequate leadership:* As noted by Corey and Corey (2006), the lack of ade-
quate training is perhaps the greatest risk. Those who are not aware of their own
biases and have little knowledge of themselves as racial and cultural beings are less
prone to develop awareness and knowledge of others (McRae & Johnson, 1991).
This lack of awareness and knowledge will make it more difficult to recognize the
boundaries of one's own multicultural competence. The risk of inadequate training is the possibility of perpetuating and colluding in situations where racial and
cultural microaggressions can do harm to group members. Although it is impossible to eliminate all possible risks in groups, it is essential that members be made
aware of potential risks and that the group worker strive to create a group environment that does not promote risks (Corey & Corey, 2006).

Summary

In this chapter, we have discussed multicultural responsibility and ethics, as well as ethical behavior such as beneficence, nonmaleficence, autonomy, justice, fidelity, and ethical issues related to the training of mental health professionals. Role clarity and leader values as well as dual relationships and informed consent have been considered. Potential psychological risks, such as self-disclosure, scapegoating, and confrontation, that need to be considered in therapeutic groups were outlined. Ethical behavior has been examined as it relates to racial-cultural dynamics in groups, noting the importance of developing competencies that include awareness, knowledge, and skills in working across differences.

QUESTIONS FOR REVIEW AND DISCUSSION

1. Referring to the case vignette presented at the beginning of the chapter, discuss the options of the student and the professor. What options do you think would be most appropriate and why?

2. What are the five principles that serve as the foundation for the ethical codes, and how are they related to working with diverse groups?

3. What is multicultural responsibility? How does it relate to ethical behavior?

4. How do the AKRI competencies contribute to our understanding of ethical behavior?

5. What are some important ethical considerations when working with group members who come from different racial cultural backgrounds?

KEY TERMS AND CONCEPTS

Autonomy	Multiculturalism and ethical guidelines
Beneficence	Nonmaleficence
Ethical issues in group work	Principles of ethical behavior
Fidelity	Psychological risks
Informed consent	Role clarity and leader values
Justice	Training
Multicultural responsibility	

WEB SITES

A. K. Rice Institute for the Study of Social Systems (AKRI): www.akriceinstitute.org

American Association for Marriage and Family Therapy (AAMFT): www.aamft.org

American Counseling Association (ACA): www.counseling.org

American Psychological Association (APA): www.apa.org

Association for Specialists in Group Work (ASGW): www.asgw.org

National Association of Social Workers (NASW): www.socialworkers.org

3

Group Formation

Racial and Cultural Dynamics
of Entering and Joining

In a small study group at a group relations conference, members were challenged by the task of discussing color and culture in the here and now. The group consisted of racially diverse members and had a white female consultant. At the beginning of the session, a white female group member initiates discussion by talking about the group's anxiety and suggests that the group establish "ground rules" for the session. Two white women question her about her comment, asking her to define the meaning of ground rules. A man of color attempts to bring the topic of race into the room by identifying the group as "mixed," and a white male validates his comment. However, after validating the existence of race in the group, the white male immediately flees from the anxiety generated by the topic. He moves the topic "outside" the group by wondering aloud about the composition of other groups that had been formed. The white female consultant addresses the group's behavior by providing an intervention that connects the group's need for ground rules with its identification of itself as a mixed group. Her intervention creates a degree of anxiety within the group that makes the members feel uncomfortable, and as a result, her comment is ignored. Immediately after the consultant's intervention, the white woman who initiated the discussion (and seems to be the group's chosen "alternate" consultant) speaks again and is again questioned by several other white women, one of whom asks "How do we become a group?" A woman of color then challenges this question by stating that she feels as if she is in a group; the white male sitting next to her agrees with her. The session continues in quite the same vein throughout, with the members speaking as if in a monologue, attempting to connect primarily by questioning or interviewing each other, alternately attacking and ignoring the consultant, and grappling with the task of talking about color, culture, and their feelings in the here-and-now experience of the group.

The scenario presented provides an example of a group in the beginning stages of formation. The interaction between the white female consultant (who represents authority within the group) and the members is characterized by the groups' reaction to her race and gender, as well as their response to the challenging task of discussing color and culture in the here and now (e.g., the need to establish ground rules in order to accomplish this task). One of the ground rules for this group seems to be the need for two simultaneous, competing narratives—that of white women members and the members of color (e.g., the "mixed" members). These narratives also represent a gender split—white women are inquirers, and males (white and "of color") are definitive statement makers. The group has also chosen an alternate consultant (e.g., another white female) to lead the group in its task of inquiry. Thus, at formation, the group has begun working openly with issues of race, gender, authority, and joining. The question asked by a female group member, "How do we become a group?" is the central question that all groups struggle with during group formation. The focus of this chapter is on racial-cultural dynamics in group formation. We use embedded intergroup relations theory (Alderfer, 1994) to understand the subgroup dynamics from the internal and external perspectives of intergroup relations. We turn to Smith and Berg's (1987) concept of paradox in groups to explore the contradiction that exists in the group-as-a-whole as it forms with members from diverse backgrounds.

An important aspect of group formation is that the group must have a function. According to Rioch (1975), "A group of people lying in the sun on a beach is not a group" (p. 22); however, she purports that when these individuals respond to the call of a drowning swimmer and attempt to rescue that person, they become a group because they now have a function. Rioch also states,

> People do not have to come together in the same room to form a group.... A hermit in the desert is inevitably a member of a group and cannot be understood unless one knows what the group is from which he has separated himself geographically. (p. 22)

We submit that when a group of individuals from different racial and cultural backgrounds come together to form a group, whatever the function, some will feel like the hermit, especially if other group members are unfamiliar and not particularly welcoming of the individual who appears to be visibly different. A person from a specific race and/or cultural background cannot be fully understood within or outside a group context without the group members having some knowledge of the group(s) that she or he has separated herself or himself from.

Embedded Intergroup Relations Theory and Group Formation

According to Alderfer's (1994) embedded intergroup relations theory, each individual reflects a uniquely related set of roles representative of an intergroup. He posits that individuals belong to multiple identity groups, including the ones they were born into such as race and gender, as well as to other groups that they choose to belong to such as professional, work, and social groups. From an external perspective, an individual may not be able to leave his or her web of group affiliations, even if he or she may want to. Embedded intergroup relations theory indicates that every transaction between two or more people depends on the unique personalities of the individuals and the messages that individuals receive and internalize from their own group. These internalized messages are characterized by the present and historical relationships between groups that certain individuals represent. Some features of this theory are (a) group boundaries that can be underdefined and too permeable, defined by Alderfer as *underbounded*, which can embody fears of abandonment in members; or group boundaries that are too rigidly defined and nonpermeable, or *overbounded*, which can elicit fears of engulfment; (b) power differences among groups, which are related to the types of institutional and systemic resources that are available to groups and how members make use of them; and (c) unconscious parallel processes of change that occur among suprasystem, system, and subsystem entities based on the assumption that "groups and organizations are open systems; that is, they both influence and are influenced by the environments in which they are embedded" (Alderfer, 1997, p. 248).

The racial-cultural dynamics of group formation are characterized by the existence of embeddedness (Alderfer, 1994); an individual's identity can be greatly affected by his or her affiliation and connectedness to his or her racial-cultural groups, which are embedded in local and a broader sociocultural context. Carter (2000) defines individuals in terms of social and cultural group membership in an organizational context and acknowledges that for some individuals group and cultural identities have salience related to both a person's self-concept as well as how others view and interact with them. Carter states that individuals seldom question their racial-cultural learning unless they encounter and/or are challenged by others whose differences conflict with their worldviews. Cultural identity is defined as manifesting itself in two ways: (1) from an individual's subjective worldview, which would encompass a variety of salient groups to which they might belong (sociocultural identity structures, such as ethnicity, social class, and political affiliations.), and (2) racial and cultural identity, which relates to visible, physical characteristics that include race, gender, skin color, hair texture, body size, attractiveness, and so on, that externally create initial impressions and predispositions, including stereotypes and prejudice. Racial-cultural identity may be embedded in other social identities such as gender, sexual orientation, age, religion, and social class, with one being more salient than the other given the situation and context. The experience that many have when joining a group is the fear of having to identify with one identity group while losing or abandoning the other. Smith and Berg (1987) refer to this dilemma as one of the paradoxes of group life.

Paradox in Groups

Smith and Berg (1987) contend that *paradox,* which they define as connections between contradictory and opposing forces, is a central theme of group life. The authors stress that group life is inherently paradoxical; contradictions exist between what people experience in groups and how these experiences are thought of and framed. Smith and Berg delineate three clusters of paradoxical group dynamics: (1) paradoxes of belonging, which refers to the complexity of membership; (2) paradoxes of engaging, which encompasses participation; and (3) paradoxes of speaking, which relates to influence. The paradox of belonging is most relevant when considering the impact of racial-cultural differences at formation. In the next section, we use the paradoxical framework to understand some of the racial-cultural dynamics that impact group formation. We use narratives from transcripts as examples of the experiences of some group members in their processes of entering and joining a group.

PARADOXES OF BELONGING

The paradox of belonging encompasses four subparadoxes: (1) individual and group identities, and the question of which identity is most salient (e.g., being a black woman involves having multiple group identities, including race, gender, sexual orientation, ability/disability, age, religion, ethnicity, and nationality); (2) involvement and detachment; (3) individuality and group norms, which continue the focus on identity and connectedness to the group and the need to maintain separateness from the group; and (4) boundaries, belonging, and not belonging to the group (Smith & Berg, 1987). The authors contend that the process of joining a group always involves coping with the anxiety of becoming a part of something that is larger than the individual self. Group members fear being accepted and not being accepted by others in the group. Being accepted could mean losing individual identity and sense of self, being involved in a group whose mission might overpower individual goals; being rejected could damage the ego, sense of self-worth, and value to the group. These are irrational fears that surface when individuals are engaged in certain groups. These are the fears that most people do not discuss except when they are in environments where it feels safe to disclose such feelings. The paradox of belonging involves the ambivalent feelings that pull a group member in two different directions at once. The boundary between the ambivalent feelings experienced as an individual, as a member of salient subgroup(s), and as a member of the group-as-a-whole create a psychological sense of belonging or not belonging.

THE PARADOX OF IDENTITY

In addition to the inherent tensions that emerge between individuals when a group is formed, the salience of racial and cultural identity can create additional tensions. For example, a group member of color who is in the minority among a group of white members might, at formation, struggle with anxieties about how his or her racial and cultural identities may be viewed by members of the group. There are both visible (race) and not readily visible aspects of racial-cultural identity (ethnicity, language, sexual orientation, religious affiliation) that can create tensions for group members at formation. Both visible or physical and not readily detectable differences can create levels of anxiety at both conscious and unconscious levels based on group members' racial prejudices, stereotypes, and fantasies. Smith and Berg (1987) state that at formation, individuals may struggle with what they might have to give up as a consequence of belonging to the group. For individuals of color, this struggle may encompass anxieties and fears about (a) how much of their racial-cultural identity they may have to fragment and abandon in order to belong and (b) what the consequences of fragmentation and abandonment may feel like, cognitively and emotionally. The question that individuals of color may ask themselves is "How much of my racial-cultural connections to family and community groups must I abandon in order to be a member of this group?" This becomes an important question and challenge for people of African, Latino/Hispanic, Asian, and American Indian descent in educational and work settings that are predominantly white, especially those with limited awareness of racial-cultural societal issues.

An African American male group member of a small study group at a group relations conference focusing on race and culture verbalizes his feelings about entering the group:

> And I'm wondering how much of that, without being rude, and I'll say that, part of that is because of the fact that I am an African American man. That there is a part of me who came, you know, if you want it, call him militant, and, had made up my mind, a long time ago, that when I came in this room, I was going to speak. And that actually, being hostile to anybody who tried to shut me down [Laughter].

Another male member responds to the group member:

> What's interesting, do you feel like anyone has tried to shut you down? Maybe that's what we can tap into, have you experienced that in this group, either overtly, or you know, unconsciously, that people are trying to silence you?

The group member responds to this question:

> I think unconsciously, yeah. Not that anyone has done anything, but, you know, it's . . . you're talking about culture. You know, my experiences, what I bring, what I brought into this room. Made, you know, I was already on guard. Because somebody might, there's someone's going to challenge me.

In this interaction, we can see that the African American man has entered the group with thoughts about joining and what that joining might entail. He entered the group with the assumption that some members would attempt to silence him. His statements are bounded by his racial and gendered identities; specifically, he expresses a concern that he had on entering this small group that he may have to fragment (e.g., bring forth) that "militant part" of himself as a result of anticipated challenges by other group members because of his race and gender. Moreover, his statements are characterized by wariness, a certain level of anxiety on entering, and about the possibility of being "shut down" or silenced by the other members. The query (or challenge) of the other male member and his inclusion of the word *unconsciously* adds depth to the level of the African American male member's response; that he himself has felt to have already been challenged by the group, unconsciously, intensifies his fears that the group will openly (e.g., consciously) attempt to shut him down. This group member, at formation, is clearly expressing a struggle concerning the salience of his identities, that is, whether the group will accept or reject him on the basis of his race and gender (Smith & Berg, 1987). Additionally, his statement indicates a keen awareness of his affiliation and connectedness to his racial-cultural group membership, as well as his experiences with how others have viewed him in the past (Alderfer, 1994, 1997; Carter, 2000). An important question to consider in this scenario is "What are his internalized messages about black men, and are they similar to or different from those held by the other members of the group?"

Other aspects of racial-cultural identity at group formation can be related to ethnicity and language fluency, as well as levels of acculturation and assimilation. At another group relations conference, a small study group with a majority of Latina/o members was formed by spending considerable time introducing themselves by sharing experiences about their names. The group members gradually began to reveal the complexity of their identities through their names:

There was a time that I was Albert. And now, I'm Alberto. I was originally (speaks in accent) Alberto and things happened and I became Albert. For me, I became Alberto. I came back home, and I was Alberto.

Fernando states,

I go from Fernando, which is my real name. Fernandito sounds like a little boy's name. So, and Fernand . . . Which works in Spanish, but in English it doesn't really work.

Alberto responds,

Right. And then I said, how come he's not Fernando? I said . . . when I saw your name.

Another member responds,

It's Fernando. I had a reaction to that too.

Another member responds,

Yeah. It's funny, when he said that, I thought wow, because I wasn't even thinking when I said it so I guess since I was mentioning before that, who do I identify with? I guess, since I grew up more with Americans or whatever, that's my name first. And before I wanted to identify as Latino, so I would always say it with a Spanish accent.

The group members continue with their focus on identity through storytelling:

I have a story. I was brought up Catholic. And when I was being baptized, my mother was asked for my name, and she says, "Fernando." The Catholic priest, who happened to be white, went into a conference and said that's not his name. That's not a real name. So my baptism certificate says Frederick. Even though that's not my name.

Another group member shares a story:

I have a student who just came into our school system, and her name is Sarah Kwan. And I said, "Where are you from?" She goes, "China." And I go, "How many people from China have a first name like Sarah?" And she said, "Well, when I came in, the guidance counselor couldn't pronounce my name, so she suggested Sarah." And I said, "What's your name?" She goes, "Hua, H-U-A." And I go, "I can [say] Hua." And then, I continued to call her Hua. And then she said to me, "I'm going to go to my counselor and change it." And she went. And she changed it to Hua again. It's easy to call somebody anything you want, but you got to try to get people to call you by your name, not the one that is easy for them to pronounce.

The group members then share their feelings about their stories:

Fernando: It's a story of pain as for the aspect of the issues around painful experiences. What's sort of hidden, I think, is something about the reality when I change one side, then one must be someone else.

Alberto: So to be part of that group, we change our name; so instead of being Alberto, we become Albert.

Arturo: To be accepted, you know. Sometimes you change your location, like the sitting arrangement in the whole group dynamic.

Alberto: Well like he said, "You wanted to be Latino before."

Fernando: Yeah.

Arturo: You know, how much do you have to change to fit in?

At the group level, the above dialogues demonstrate the paradox of inclusion and exclusion based on conformity to Western cultural values and sensibilities.

The group members move through a process of formation that is bounded by the complexity of their multiple identities, symbolized by narratives about their names. The sharing of these narratives of names (their own as well as those of individuals outside the group) is characterized by their experiences with racism, discrimination, and prejudice at a societal level and is also related to their need to explore levels of language fluency, acculturation, and assimilation within the group. They also explore the pain inherent in the paradox of identity—the necessity of fragmenting their identities to become a part of the group-as-a-whole.

Falicov (1998) states that among Latinas/os in the United States, "There is much in a name" (p. 96); experiences of racism, discrimination, and prejudice have resulted in name changes that reflect historical trends toward inclusion or exclusion, ethnic affirmation, or shame and a wish to assimilate to the dominant culture or isolate from it. Choices that Latinas/os, Asians, and other immigrants make to deny their own names and language (all of which are intricately tied to their identity) may stem from experiences of racism and discrimination, and a wish to avoid group and societal exclusion.

THE PARADOX OF INVOLVEMENT

Exploration of a group member's involvement in a group at formation encompasses the paradox of involvement and withdrawal, which is characterized by detachment, observation, and experience (Smith & Berg, 1987). Group members may struggle with levels of commitment to themselves and to the group as a way of managing how much they will be involved in the group. They may begin to consciously and unconsciously explore concerns and fears of belonging, while simultaneously avoiding being engulfed (Wells, 1985) by the group. The challenge that group members are confronted with is fear of engulfment by the group (e.g., a subgroup) and a loss of certain aspects of self. Anxieties that individual group members have concerning race and culture may complicate the paradox of involvement: Group members of color may detach, observe, and experience group dynamics through a racial-cultural lens. Racial-cultural group affiliation and anxieties about identity during formation can lead to detached and withdrawing behaviors for some individuals of color in the group. Thus, the threat of engulfment by the group at formation may threaten an individual's sense of the salience of their racial-cultural identities and their ability to fully enter the group. Alternatively, other members' reactions to these detaching behaviors may inhibit the group's ability to move forward. For instance, in the previous example, the male group member's question about whether or not the African American man had experienced the group as silencing him was reflective of a group concern, possibly about racist tendencies among members. As the group progresses, members could, because of feelings of anxiety, guilt, and shame, flee from all dialogues about race and culture or engage with more caution, which would ultimately be counterproductive to their process of involvement.

Smith and Berg (1987) assert that the ability to be involved is intricately tied to the ability to be removed and that reflection informs action and action informs reflection. Both the individual group member and the group-as-a-whole must attempt the difficult task of getting "outside of one's experience while at the same time remaining inside that experience" (p. 97). Thus, in the example above, the African American man and the group are involved while at the same time keeping parts of themselves removed from involvement. The Latino group members speak of their experiences of having to change their names outside the group while claiming and holding on to their names in the group. Will the members from the dominant racial-cultural group be able to be involved with the authentic Latinos who have joined this group? Can they hold on to their racial-cultural identity and still belong to the group?

THE PARADOX OF INDIVIDUALITY

The paradox of individuality involves the need for individuality and the pull to participate in the survival of the group (Smith & Berg, 1987). An expression of individuality on the part of a member without an understanding of the group's identity can be unwise, even dangerous to the sense of belonging desired by the member for the group; the more natural response is to be cautious, to withhold energies, wishes, and secrets until one feels more secure within the group. Such caution is also related to fears of losing parts of oneself or identity to the group. The paradox, however, is that withholding individuality makes the group unsafe:

> A group can become a group only when individuals put themselves into it, for it is the contributions of individuals that enable connections among people to form, connections that become woven into a fabric from which the foundation of the group is constructed. (Smith & Berg, 1987, p. 100)

For individuals from different racial and cultural groups, joining a group involves coping with issues of identity fragmentation and struggles with levels of involvement. Because of the tension and anxiety created by these dynamics, individuals may choose to sacrifice expressions of individuality as a consequence of attaining membership. Group members can view an individual's race and culture as an indicator of a member's individuality, positively or negatively. In addition to visible markers of difference related to skin color, expressing one's individuality in a group can take many forms (e.g., expressions of competence/incompetence, personal beliefs, likes/dislikes, agreements/disagreements) and can reveal previously hidden aspects of group members' personality and behavior. The risk inherent in self-expression within the group is of receiving projections and being cast into a particular role, for example, that of a leader or a victim to be scapegoated. Race and culture can influence the type of projections placed on a group member and the role(s) that they begin to take up in service of the group. For example, one of the cultural myths about African American women is that they are strong and frequently angry. Thus, an African American and/or black woman who expresses her individuality passionately in the form of ideas and opinions that may conflict with those of other members may be viewed as negative and/or coming from a stance of anger and hostility. Black women in group settings may feel simultaneously familiar and frustrated with the role of the "angry black woman." Groups and systems may also exert a seductive pull on black women to engage in racial dialogue and express anger and hostility on behalf of the group. Cultural myths about Asian women include labels of submissiveness and passivity; thus, an Asian woman who is more silent than other group members may be perceived as a passive and nonparticipating member. Depending on ethnicity, generation status, as well as levels of acculturation and assimilation, Asian women may be more interdependent (as opposed to individualistic) and may therefore have a tendency to focus on the needs of the group as opposed to attending to their own needs, independent to those of the group. Group members, especially those from disenfranchised groups, are usually keenly aware of cultural myths and the dangers inherent in self-expression of individuality in groups in which they are the minority (McRae et al., 2007).

Expressions of individuality can foster connections and disconnections in a group, both jeopardizing and strengthening the group. Additionally, for group members, taking the risk of expressing differences and similarities supports and threatens their own individuality (Smith & Berg, 1987). A female group member expresses her anxieties about individuality:

> That actually speaks to my experience that I studied, not really in this group, but in many that I've been in, about race and culture, where, normally, in a task group, I'm a leader. I'll be like, this is what you do. And, I'll just run the entire thing from beginning to end. But when it's a group about culture, and, race, and ethnicity, all of a sudden I've, and it's frustrating, but I fall into the role of an Asian female being quiet, and I just recently have learned this about myself, and even here, and it's not anything that I can identify that anybody's done, and that it is so much of what I bring into it, and, now I realize, oh, these are the stereotypes of being Asian, and female. And then I fall into the role. And that's how I experience myself. And I knew this would happen. And I am seeing it happening in this group, where I become a little bit more quiet. And much more . . . submissive than I usually am.

Another member makes an inquiry about her statement:

> Do you think we're doing that?

The woman responds,

> I really don't think so, but at the same time, when I first realized it, it was in another group where culture and race was talked about very intensely. And I started deferring to all the white people. And at, what that had to do with . . . reflections on every class, and it wasn't until half way through that, I realized, why am I asking all of the people in community what do they think, or, am I right? Or, so, it just happened, and unconsciously, either on my part, or on the group's part, I have no idea, and even right now, I have no idea.

This group member's statements reveal her struggle with expressing her individuality, her competence as a leader, and her awareness and frustration with cultural myths about Asian women in predominantly white systems. She is also expressing the tension she feels between her individuality and the pull of the group on her to behave in stereotypical ways that may be more familiar to the group (e.g., to be silent, passive, and submissive).

THE PARADOX OF BOUNDARIES

The paradox of boundaries is that they "both constrain and release, restrict and enable, contain and create anxiety" (Berg & Smith, 1990, p. 117). Boundaries are integral to multiple aspects of groups; at formation (and throughout the group's life) boundaries can determine group affiliation (e.g., who's in and who's out of the group), concrete boundaries of starting and ending, spatial boundaries related to location, and less visible boundaries, such as the psychological sense that individuals develop of belonging to the group as members and their awareness of group norms (e.g., what is acceptable and unacceptable to the group) (Smith & Berg, 1987).

Boundaries function as containers that hold the groups' anxieties of membership by providing appropriate space and time for engagement and dialogue about the anxieties experienced by the group. Effective boundaries provide a containing effect that can allow for powerful experiences on the part of group members. Boundaries are, in essence, both the life and the death of the group: If they are too loose or poorly defined, the group may not survive because of excessive influences from the outside. Boundaries that are too rigid and closed off to the external environment may lead to the group feeding on its own anxieties, isolating itself from the external world, until it becomes unbearable for the members (Smith & Berg, 1987).

The psychological aspect of boundaries is most relevant to the racial-cultural affiliation and the identities of group members. Because of subgroup affiliations and experiences with discrimination and marginalization at the societal level, group members of color may have familiarity with the experience of managing multiple levels of belonging. Their knowledge of group norms, for example, may be affected by a hypervigilant awareness of what is acceptable and unacceptable to the group, as well as the consequences involved in behavior that transgresses group norms. The African American male group member who was concerned even before joining his group about being challenged for speaking was dealing with the boundary paradox of containing or creating anxiety in the group. Should he constrain himself or release his feelings? How would it affect other group members and his relationship with them? The Latina/Latino group members who explored the difficult and sometimes painful experience of changing one's identity to fit in and be accepted were dealing with the paradox of restricting and enabling themselves and the group. Would claiming their identity create restrictions in the managing of group boundaries, or would it enable the group to be more inclusive and engaging of cultural differences? Finally, the Asian American female group member who struggled with maintaining her identity as a leader while also experiencing the seductive pull of the group to conform to a stereotyped role struggled with one of the complexities of the psychological boundaries of membership. How could she hold on to her identity and not give in to a stereotypic role? The need to belong is a natural human quality; most human beings desire contact with others. At the same time, when joining a group, the fear of simultaneously belonging and losing important aspects of self creates ambivalent emotions that can cause feelings of being pulled in two opposing directions, with positive and negative attributes on each side.

Summary

This chapter has focused on racial-cultural dynamics of group formation, specifically, the processes of entering and joining. The theories of embedded intergroup relations (Alderfer, 1994) and the paradoxes of belonging (Smith & Berg, 1987) have been reviewed and explored as they relate to racial-cultural dynamics of group formation. Examples of small study groups at conferences have been provided to illustrate the complexity of entering and joining for group members.

QUESTIONS FOR REVIEW AND DISCUSSION

1. How are race and culture connected to group formation?

2. What is embedded intergroup relations theory?

3. What is meant by the term *paradox in groups*?

4. Describe the paradoxes of belonging.

5. Create a scenario that can serve as an example of paradox in groups where the members are from different racial-cultural backgrounds (use your own as well as others' experiences).

KEY TERMS AND CONCEPTS

Embedded intergroup relations theory

Group formation

Paradox in groups

Paradox of boundaries, belonging and not belonging

Paradox of individual identity and group identity

Paradox of individuality and group norms

Paradox of involvement and detachment

Paradoxes of belonging

4

Group Development

The Impact of Racial and Cultural Factors

G roup development theory helps those who study groups to anticipate events that occur during the life span of the group to identify phases of interpersonal activity or dynamic processes in which group members engage. Such theory describes the patterns of growth and change that occur in groups from the time of formation to dissolution. According to theories of group development, the group moves through a number of phases or emotional states while doing its work of surviving and thriving as a functional unit. The group moves through a dynamic process as members become oriented and test each other and the facilitator or consultant while developing and negotiating rules of engagement (Tuckman, 1965). Members experience feelings of dependency on the facilitator for structure and assurance that the group will be safe enough to attain the group's goals. If the leader is not perceived as meeting the group's needs, members will search for other leadership in the group and will feel a sense of frustration if there is no alternative leader or savior who emerges to save the group from inevitable disaster. These are just a few ways of exploring the dynamic processes that develop among individuals who come together and form a group.

This chapter addresses the following questions: How is group development affected by the racial-cultural differences of its members? How do racial-cultural dynamics influence the ways in which the group develops? How are group member relationships and power differentials influenced by racial-cultural factors that are manifested in both overt and covert ways during the life of the group? How do the social context, historical relationships between subgroups, internalized messages, and biases of members affect the group's development? First, we briefly review three models of group development (see Smith, 2001, for a more in-depth review); then, racial-cultural issues in group development will be addressed.

Models of Group Development

Models of group development address the personal dynamics of individual group members and the dynamics and functioning of the group as an entity (Bennis & Shepard, 1974; Hare, 1976; Mills, 1967; Tuckman, 1965; Tuckman & Jensen, 1977). Each model of group development identifies a stage, phase, or mode that the group enters to deal with certain interpersonal and task issues. Group development models have been classified into three categories: linear or progressive models, cyclical models, and nonsequential models (Mennecke, Hoffer, & Wynn, 1992; Smith, 2001). Conceptually, whether the group is considered to be progressing linearly from one stage to another or moving cyclically or nonsequentially, the group must deal with relationships between its members; with the designated leader, facilitator, or consultant; and with issues of power and boundaries.

PROGRESSIVE MODELS

Progressive theorists (Bennis & Shepard, 1974; Mills, 1967; Tuckman, 1965; Tuckman & Jensen, 1977) propose that the group moves through a number of stages, resolving one issue before moving onto the next. Bennis and Shepard (1974) contend that the principal obstacles to valid communication in groups are related to member orientation toward authority and intimacy. Authority relations are connected to dependency, while intimacy or personal relations are connected to interdependence in the group. Groups with members who depend on authorities to provide direction and who have difficulty trusting their own ability to foster group movement tend to be more conflicted, whereas groups with a mixture of dependent and counterdependent members will work toward interdependence and independence, which ultimately make for more effectively functioning groups (Bennis & Shepard, 1974). Other theorists (Kuypers, Davies, & Hazewinkel, 1986) have noted that in addition to authority and intimacy, inclusion is a concern for members as the group develops. Each member enters the group with feelings about joining; there is a wish for acceptance and concern about being rejected. When a member sees himself or herself as a minority in the group, the fear of rejection or lack of acceptance may increase; this depends on the prior experiences of the member in groups or similar situations. Working with and across differences is also related to the internal messages learned about self, one's social identity group(s), cultural values, and the historical relatedness between the subgroups represented in the group.

As stated previously, Tuckman (1965) and Tuckman and Jensen's (1977) stages (*forming, storming, norming, performing,* and *adjourning*) incorporate most of the other models. In the *forming* stage, the group process involves an orientation to the task or the basic criteria for the group's existence. Members work at different levels of intensity on inclusion in the group; there is a sense of dependency, confusion, ambiguity, and anxiety when the group does not have clear guidance from someone with authority about what is to occur in the group. There is also a testing of boundaries in the group regarding what is acceptable and unacceptable behavior. In the *storming* stage, the group is in conflict with the leaders and one another; usually there is a sense of members being polarized into camps on different sides of an issue. The group deals with conflicts of power and decision making, such as who is in charge, and whether or not they can trust the authority and leadership of the group. There is a general resistance to task and to group influence, which allows members to work through some of their control issues. During this phase of group development, the group tends to resolve its dependence on authority through rebellion. Rebellion can be exhibited by behaviors of ignoring interventions made by the group facilitator, for example, by questioning whether their comments are relevant or irrelevant to the discussion. The *norming* stage involves the development of group cohesion, a sharing of personal narratives, and the establishment of group norms. Members adopt new roles and standards for group behavior, and there is an appreciation for the group and its task. The members explore more functional relationships in a collaborative manner. The *performing* stage occurs when the group has resolved interpersonal conflict and found ways to be more collaborative. In this stage, roles become more flexible and functional, and the group is able to channel its energy toward achieving the task. The last stage, *adjourning*, is the termination of the group; members are faced with the enrichment and learning from the group, as well as the lost opportunities for certain interpersonal and group exchanges that were considered by members but never acted on. There is usually a combination of happy, sad, angry, and/or ambivalent feelings about the overall group experience.

CYCLICAL MODELS

According to the cyclical model, groups revisit different stages or phases of the group, depending on the issues that surface in the group at a given time, which could be related to changes in the group membership or to external and environmental concerns (Smith, 2001). The cyclical model theorists (Bales & Strodtbeck, 1951; Hare, 1976; Napier & Gershenfeld, 1973; Schultz, 1958; Stock & Thelen, 1958) identify a number of phases that groups work through to function effectively. Schultz's (1958) model focuses on interpersonal issues of the group. He postulates that the group develops through three phases that are recurring: *inclusion, control,* and *affection.* Napier and Gershenfeld (1973) identify five phases: (1) *beginning,* (2) *movement toward confrontation,* (3) *compromise and harmony,* (4) *reassessment,* and (5) *resolution and recycling.* One way to think about the cyclical model is as a pendulum, swinging from one issue to the next, depending on the issues that arise among the members in the context of the group. Usually these issues are related to boundaries, relationships, and power. Bion's (1961) work on basic assumption groups, which is considered by some to fit into the developmental cyclical model, is not being included here because he did not write it with that intent, and others have written that he "explicitly rejected the possibility of placing these assumptions in the developmental context" (Gibbard, Hartman, & Mann, 1974, p. 86). We consider Bion's work as the foundation for the dynamic processes in groups, which is the focus of Chapter 5. However, the dynamics described by Bion (dependency, fight/flight, and pairing) are captured in each of the developmental phases, cycles, and nonsequential models discussed here. The cyclical model of group development offers a more dynamic approach to understanding group development. In the cyclical model, the group is constantly assessing new experiences and emotions that develop and addresses them, as opposed to the more rigid structure of linear group development. In our experience, the more flexible cyclical model is often helpful in understanding racial and cultural factors in group development.

NONSEQUENTIAL MODELS

The nonsequential models of group development do not have a prescribed pattern for group development (Smith, 2001). There are five nonsequential models: (1) Poole's contingency model, (2) McGrath's time interaction and performance model (TIP), (3) the punctuated equilibrium model by Gersick, (4) the dynamic contingency model by McCollom, and (5) the TEAM model, a description of team development by Morgan, Salas, and Glickman (see Smith, 2001). These models purport that groups develop in nonsequential ways depending on a number of environmental factors, time, emotional processes in the group, tasks, roles, authority structures, member characteristics, relationships, and topical issues. According to these models, groups might start at one phase and come back to one that is considered an earlier phase, depending on where the group is in relation to its tasks and emotional states. For instance, in the contingency model, the group is seen as dealing with three intertwining threads that evolve simultaneously: (1) task process behavior, (2) work relationships, and (3) topical focus (Smith, 2001). McCollom (1990) presented the dynamic contingency model as an alternative to other models because she views group development as a dynamic process that develops over time and that is contingent on a variety of complex factors.

RECURRING ISSUES

Each of the group development models proposes three primary psychological issues that every group must deal with during its life. The issues relate to (1) member concerns about boundaries, (2) relationships, and (3) power. In our experience, these recurring dynamics are manifested in either blatant or subtler ways in a wide variety of groups. Tuckman's (1965) progressive model captures the pattern of emotional states that groups move through, even when the process is not linear. The cyclical and nonsequential models of group development offer a more flexible and adaptive format for what actually occurs in groups, especially those that are racially and culturally mixed.

Racial and Cultural Issues in Groups

Group development models suggest that there is a universal pattern of how groups develop and provide little insight about how racial-cultural dynamics between members affect the group's movement in working with and through the various phases. The assumption is that when individuals come together as a group, regardless of their racial-cultural backgrounds, similar dynamic processes occur. There is a dearth of research and literature on group development with diverse racial-cultural groups, especially therapeutic groups. In our experience working with diverse racial-cultural groups, we have found that it is important to help individuals become more aware of the boundaries, power issues, and relatedness of the group members. Boundary issues tend to be more prominent in the early life of a group. Once established, the group develops a sense of security and containment that allows members to work on other issues. Power issues, while relevant initially in the group, are more difficult to discuss and usually surface as the members get to know each other a little better. Relationships begin to develop early between and among members, but it can take some time for members to experience a connection that can sustain relational tensions. Addressing boundaries, power, and relational issues helps the group process and manage the paradox of belonging and not belonging that was discussed in Chapter 3. In diverse racial-cultural groups, these issues are a part of group members' lived experience and are manifested in a variety of complex ways in the group. Group workers can help members become more aware of how these issues affect relatedness.

BOUNDARIES: DRAWING THE LINES

During the initial phase of group formation, members are more aware of racial and ethnic differences and are more likely to draw on stereotypes and biases from information learned from their own racial or ethnic groups or past interactions (Brown & Mistry, 1994; McRae, 1994; Tsui & O'Reilly, 1989). The visible differences of race and ethnicity in most instances are obvious but are often unspeakable; they become the "pink elephant" in the middle of the room. Members become more aware of the invisible differences such as sexual orientation, social class, and religion as they interact. Racial and ethnic subgroup boundaries are often drawn in the form of member alliances for support and protection from feared attacks and, depending on the composition of the group, for acquisition of power.

When individuals from different racial-cultural backgrounds come together to form a group, whether it is a therapy, self-analytic, or work group, there are a number of possible concerns or issues that they may need to manage in order to develop into a functional group. We use the term *functional* broadly to mean a group that is taking up its task and finding ways to work effectively that are specific to that group, given the context in which they exist. Members come with stereotypes and perceptions of their own and other groups. Members come with cultural belief systems and social class statuses that prescribe relationships and power differences within and between racial and ethnic groups.

In terms of racial preferences for group composition, white participants tend to prefer to be in groups that are predominantly white, and black participants tend to select groups that are composed of equal numbers of blacks and whites (Davis & Burnstein, 1981). Li, Karakowsky, and Siegel (1999) did a study of proportional representation on intragroup behavior in mixed-race groups' decision making and found that Asians, when in the numerical minority position, were significantly more passive and introverted than when in same-race groups. McPherson and Smith-Lovin (1987) used the term *homophily,* which is defined as a tendency for people to be attracted to people with similar attitudes, beliefs, and personal characteristics. There are others who concur that similar people tend to join groups with similar people and value the contributions of those who are similar more than those who are dissimilar (see Brown & Mistry, 1994; McPherson & Smith-Lovin, 1987; Tsui & O'Reilly, 1989).

Boundary differences, which are physical and psychological, may be unspeakable in the group, but that does not mean that members are not aware of them. Race and culture are physical boundaries that are potentially dangerous to talk about, depending on members' personal characteristics. Certain members may have never encountered someone from another racial or ethnic group and may use stereotypic assumptions in their interactions that can create tensions that are never spoken about in the group. For example, the immigrant who has recently relocated to a new country and does not speak English fluently may not be understood by others, but in group settings may rarely be asked to repeat what he or she has said. As presented in the vignette at the beginning of Chapter 2, the other group members might act as if they understand or merely ignore what the person has said.

The psychological boundaries that are less visible often involve authority dynamics, available resources, and relationships between subgroups

(Alderfer, 1994). Racial-cultural boundaries also create a sense of members being polarized into camps on different sides of an issue. When the group has just formed, polarization can get acted out in a number of ways. In one small study group that consisted of all people of color, half black and half Asian, two of the black women decided that the door needed to be closed so that the group could begin its work. Usually, in these study groups, the consultant enters the room at the time boundary or beginning of the group and shuts the door before sitting. A black woman was the consultant for the group; she had entered and shut the door, and a member came in after her, leaving the door open. The group members exhibited some anxiety about whether or not to begin, and when the consultant did not get up and close the door, a black woman group member decided to take up the authority to begin the group. The black and Asian women in the group had the following exchange:

Mary (Black Woman):	Could you close the door? [Laughter]
	[Asian man gets up and closes the door.]
Agnes (Asian Woman):	I was thinking, we could leave it open until she comes.
Mary:	Oh.
Linda (Black Woman):	When we start is determined by the members; that's not the criteria for when the party starts, like we show up. So, then the door should be closed for the time.
Joy (Asian Woman):	I can see it the other way too, like usually we wait for everyone to come.
Agnes:	I mean, it's not like a big deal, but, you know . . . okay. Maybe she was just running late.
Mary:	Well, we're here.
Agnes:	The thought just occurred to me about waiting for her to come, and how that was kind of important to me. I think it reflects the value of the collective. I don't know, I just thought of that, just came to my mind, the importance of being whole, and a group.
Linda:	Well, you know, it is kind of interesting that the group removed a woman of African descent, I mean a black woman, the group dismissed one. I don't know what that means, but this group . . . exited a woman of African descent. . . .

In this scenario, the black women group members joined to close the door on behalf of the black woman consultant. They wanted to abide by the time boundaries and start the group at the appointed time. The Asian women used their cultural values as a way of countering the African American women group members' management of the time boundary, introducing an alternative idea of what the cultural norm of the group would be. The question that challenged the group was "Which norms would prevail?" Would the group norm set by the Western model of group relations, which values a more rigid management of boundaries, as espoused by the consultant (and the directorate of the conference), be adhered to? Or was there room for other cultural values and norms, which were more inclusive and accommodating for the member who was late? One of the African American women switched the focus from culture to race, stating that the group had exited a woman of African descent. The struggle for control of the group was centered on culture and race, two factors that held salience for each of these identity groups. The Asians claimed that in their culture, which is collective, they believe in waiting for the entire group to gather. A young Asian man, who had closed the door, joined in the confrontation, using cultural values as the rationale for understanding the difference, and implied that the black women were missing a national cultural base, an identifiable country with a distinct culture, rather than just a continent connection.

As the group was forming, there were some feelings of dependency on the consultant as the authority figure in the room to close the door and signal the time boundary to begin the group; when this did not occur, the black female members took up that authority on her behalf, while simultaneously blaming the group for aggressive behavior toward a black woman. While still in the formation stage, this group was also dealing with storming, or what Bion (1961) identified as the fight/flight emotional phase of group life. Their desire for direction from the consultant created tension in the group, which was indicated by the members' argument about shutting out a member, who was responsible, and what it meant for the group to have done this. They spent time exploring differing cultural belief systems, collective versus independent, until the missing member arrived and announced that she was African Latina. In this group, the presence of multiple Asian members may have served to strengthen their collective voice and power; this did not occur in other groups where there were fewer Asian members. This is consistent with the work of Cheng, Chae, and Gunn (1998) and Tsui (1997). Tsui (1997) suggests that lack of clear boundaries between the authority figure and group members may cause Asian clients to worry about who is in charge. In this group, they were activated to challenge others members of color for leadership.

The above work is supported by research conducted by Shaw and Barrett-Power (1998), who explored the effects of diversity on small-work-group development and developed a model that correlated attributes of various characteristics, those that are readily detectable, such as race, ethnicity, and gender, and those that are underlying, such as cultural values, beliefs, paradigm dissimilarity, and skills in managing differences. They report that visible differences, as well as those that are invisible but are detected through interpersonal exchange, cause individuals to become more aware of their social identity (or identities), creating a sense of "me and not me," which activates stereotypic and biased interpretations of others' behavior. Judgments or decisions are then more likely to be inaccurate, affect interactions negatively, and increase anxiety.

Thus, for multicultural groups to work productively at the various emotional phases of group development, they need to have some members who are motivated to participate in mixed groups, who have a level of self-esteem and self-confidence, who are open to dealing with differences, and who have some awareness of how their behavior affects others. These characteristics will enhance the members' capacity to work with group boundaries, relationships, and power issues that are bound to surface in the group, because of individual personalities, the messages the individuals receive and internalize from their own racial-cultural groups, and histories of relatedness of the racial-cultural groups represented and carried by members (Alderfer, 1994). When groups are mixed racially, ethnically, and culturally (just to name a few), subgroups exist in which members may hold multiple connections to either an identity group such as race, ethnicity, religion, or sexual orientation or to an organizational group (e.g., attending the same school, working for the same agency, professional groups).

THE FIGHT FOR POWER

Power and privilege are what members struggle with in all types of groups. Who has power and privilege and who does not? How can those who do not have it get it, and will those who have it share or give it up? Racial-cultural differences and the intragroup histories of oppressor and oppressed create a situation that is even more complex. When confronted with these issues, the group may go into the fight/flight mode described by Bion (1961). Tuckman (1965) referred to this as the storming stage of group development and Schultz (1958) as control. The fight/flight mode represents the group's desire to preserve itself regardless of the differences. Thus, members can fight about who has more power, resources, and privileges, or they can act as if these differences do not exist or are not important to them, during this phase of the group members' struggle with the paradox of belonging and not belonging. The issue of "me and not me" becomes central in terms of decision making and influence in the group. There is a push for resolution of ambivalent feelings and, simultaneously, a wish to gain or maintain control over topics of discussion. In some groups, however, the experience may feel more like a conflict that will never be resolved or that members are stuck.

A general hypothesis that can be drawn from Shaw and Barrett-Power's (1998) research on diverse work groups is that race, ethnicity, personal attitudes, cultural values, beliefs, and styles of conflict resolution will be negatively related to group effectiveness during the initial phases of group development because of the costs of working with the complexity of differences for many individuals. They suggest that the group will have more difficulty resolving conflict because of these differences. These authors propose that the differences in group members can be managed more effectively when the members have developed multicultural competence. Members with high self-esteem and self-confidence who are willing to develop relationships and communicate with others who are different from them and have an understanding of how their own behavior might affect others will have less anxiety in diverse groups.

Ideally, members who join a group with diverse membership will have had some exposure to other racial-cultural groups. However, this is not always the case; thus, groups in which members have not yet developed multicultural competence must be effectively led by group workers. In groups with members who have undeveloped levels of multicultural competence, members may question the value or purpose of the group and may act as if they do not hear or understand the interventions of the leader. This type of behavior is evidence of their resistance to the anxiety of working with the complex attitudes and perceptions they have about working with differences.

Power in the group can be manifested in a number of different ways. For example, in a small study group that was predominantly Latino, as presented in Chapter 3, the Latino members began the group with a long discussion about how several of them had gotten their names changed when they came to the United States, either by teachers or priests who had difficulty saying their names. The other members of the group, who were not Latino, sat and listened but did not engage in the discussion. After about 20 minutes, the consultant to the group, who was Latino, commented on who was talking and who was not and wondered if it was a statement about who held the power to determine the focus of the conversation in the group. The Latino members were able to control the topic by taking flight from their here-and-now experience to their past experiences as immigrants. It served as a way of bonding the Latino subgroup that had been oppressed by white people in powerful positions, thus making clear the "me and not me" in the group. It was also an opportunity for the Latino members to hold and demonstrate their power in the group. When the consultant addressed the dynamic, the members were able to discuss what happened and their feelings about it. The Latino members spoke of how great it felt to have been able to acknowledge the power in their numbers and the rarity of this experience in an institutional and group setting.

In a predominantly white gay and lesbian small study group, the members pulled for the consultant, a tall, large-framed, openly gay black man, to make his sexual orientation central in connecting to them. One white male member spoke to his fears of the power of a large, black male, referring to fears of potential aggression, hostility, and abuse of his power. The group was unable to work with this dynamic for some time. They instead focused their anger on the one Latina woman in the group who sat silently, refusing to engage with the group. The consultant commented that he wondered if the group was really angry at him for not being more responsive but found the Latina member to be an easier target at whom to vent their anger, since she was the member who looked most like him, in terms of skin color. This direct confrontation to the group about their behavior changed the members' focus from trying to get the young woman to talk to an expression of their feelings and fantasies about the consultant, his power, and how it affected the group.

When members are more able to recognize and openly discuss privileges afforded them by race, gender, ethnicity, sexual orientation, and so on, the group works more effectively toward its task. In the following example, a young white man challenges others in the group to talk more about the complexity that exists in the room and states that he will not apologize for being a white man:

> There is a complexity in this room and we're not dealing with it. I don't know how to deal with it. That was fine. But, I guess I was just getting very defensive about this sandwich between two white men. I can, I'm not going to apologize for my genes that, I popped out of a white woman. That's how I was born. I can't . . . I feel like, I think that beneath a lot of what we're saying are these implicit and unconscious apologies.

His comment speaks to the intense feelings of guilt and shame about belonging to one group and not another. The attempts to redress social justice referred to by Reed and Noumair (2000) are mythical and cannot be easily resolved. It is the recognition and work at understanding "the other" that creates the foundation for connecting and a sense of belonging in the group.

When the group members are from different racial and ethnic backgrounds, the conflict could be about cultural values, race, language, or oppression. The subgroup boundaries serve as a defensive mode for competition between subgroups, while affective patterns and cognitive distortions attributed to certain racial groups ignite negative perceptions and biases as a form of justification for emotions and behaviors. Talking openly about differences creates space to work with the common issues that surface in this phase of groups, such as competition, jealousy, envy and caring, and loving, which are all potentially taboo to verbalize in group settings. Sometimes in racially diverse groups, race and culture are used as cover stories that mask the underlying competition in the group. Members may struggle to talk about their racial-cultural differences, but these differences are often only one part of the group dynamic.

Members may feel shame or guilt about feelings of jealousy and envy toward someone who has certain earned/unearned privileges or power, whether the person is white or of color. In these instances, the group leader must explore both racial-cultural factors and the dynamics related to competition. It is important to let group members know that it is natural and productive to have these feelings and to emphasize the difference between having and expressing feelings and acting on what they may feel. The group leader must communicate to the group that the expression of feelings often prevents dysfunctional acting out behaviors.

RELATIONSHIPS: MOVING CLOSER, UNDERSTANDING MORE

When the group has come to some resolution with their differences, they become more prepared to address relational concerns. While both processes (working with differences and relationships) complement each other, they are not necessarily linear; we address them separately for clarity. To become intimate, members need to make authentic connections and feel that the group environment is a safe enough container for them to express feelings and not be punished. Members may then develop a better understanding of the roles they take up in the group and have more insight about the group's processes. They become more invested in the work of the group, and the group environment feels more productive and therapeutic (Kline, 2003). Members are more willing to share personal information, take risks, and confront others in the group without fear of being ostracized. According to Tuckman (1965), this phase of the group's development would be called *norming and performing;* Bennis and Shepard (1974) would call it *enchantment, disenchantment, and consensual validation,* in which the group engages in interpersonal dilemmas of intimacy and members connect with one another. The group establishes a norm for member behavior that is acceptable and works in a productive manner on interpersonal and group concerns. In the following example, members from a study group began to talk about their attraction to each other. There were two openly gay men in the group and a heterosexual, middle-aged Jewish man whom the women reached out to in different ways.

Woman: I hear that, accept that—and you're saying. My attraction to Gary (black gay male) and to Michael (white gay male) is they're both— their bald heads. I would love to be able to touch their bald head[s]. It's a very sensual thing for me. You know? It's a very sensual thing, and I feel very safe with them. I feel safe. And there is something in me that—what is it that makes me feel safe with gay men? Why do I feel safe in my home with my husband, who has a sexual issue? You know? Who can't—in my mind, in my own thinking, I want him to be gay. Like it's me who's saying, "I want you to be gay because I'm safe then. I'm safe."

Man: Is the safety not looking at your own sexuality?

Woman: I've been molested myself. You know? So I'm safe with a gay man. You know? So I want him to be gay. I am protective of him.

Another woman joins the conversation to express her attraction to the middle-aged heterosexual Jewish man in the group:

Woman #2: Part of the bizarreness or compounding bizarreness for me is that I've never felt so uncomfortable in my life. My attraction to you, Jerry, as a father figure, and there's [something else]. I know, I know.

In this group, the move toward intimacy is initiated by the women in their desire to touch or get close to the men who are safe because they are not perceived as being available to them sexually. This type of intimacy was also safe for the men in the group, who responded that they appreciated the comments, except for the Jewish man, who was a little surprised that he was being perceived as a father figure.

The tensions in groups about power and relationships are continuous and healthy for the life of the group if space exists to talk and tensions are relieved. When there is limited or no space for discussion and sharing, there is no outlet and the tension builds and may, at times, feel explosive. Creating space for expression of differences in groups is a powerful element of group work. Members must feel that the leader of the group will support and work with them in a nonjudgmental way. In our work with groups, we often purposely acknowledge at the start of the group that everyone has biases, emphasizing that it is the process of becoming aware of them and how they might affect the lives of others that helps group leaders create productive group work environments.

Terminating the Group

According to group development theory, all groups must deal with termination of the group's life. Group endings are a metaphor for other endings in life and are an important aspect of the group's learning. Groups end in many different ways: They have attained their goal, resolved the issues that surfaced, performed the tasks necessary or required, and, it is hoped that the groups have developed some form of intimacy between members. Of course, some groups achieve these goals and some do not. Members often spend the last session asking for feedback from others, something to carry away in remembrance and growth. At other times, there is no request for feedback and it feels like members just want to leave and forget about the entire experience. The life of the group is dynamic and depends on the personalities, messages internalized about self, the histories of relatedness among members that create the group environment, and, ultimately, how members adjourn. In the following example, two members who had a difficult encounter concerning their ethnic differences earlier in the group attempt to connect and understand their differences as generational.

Man: I'm also a Jew in my 50s, and thus I have a whole history and a connection to a Germany that is very unlike the Germany you come from.

Woman: And I would again say, not being disrespectful, like please don't get this wrong, but, again, so, because I'm a whole new generation.

Man: I know. But I need to learn about that.

Woman: Yeah.

Man: And that's something that maybe you can teach me. But at the same time, you have to take in my projection about what it provokes in me. I still come from a generation that has experienced considerable anti-Semitism. Some of it was in Germany, actually.

Woman: Yeah. I believe that.

Man: I mean so all I'm trying to say—I'm trying to share a part of myself; I'm trying to connect with you. I'm trying to ask you for something, as well, but I'm also using it as an example of that there are data that we have about each other that we're not using, and we're not connecting.

In this vignette, the Jewish man and German woman are working to create a connection that they were not able to make earlier, possibly because of the many internalized messages that they have of their respective social identity groups as well as experiences of oppression and their own personality styles. This type of encounter is not unusual at the end of the group. Members want to leave feeling good about their group experience. They want to make amends with those they have been in conflict with and leave with positive feelings. The group leader's role during termination is to allow sufficient time for members to work on issues of termination and to help members recognize what they have gained or learned from the experience.

Summary

In this chapter, we have reviewed group development theories and racial-cultural factors in group development. Three models of group development theory (progressive, cyclical, and nonsequential) were briefly reviewed, and then we discussed racial and cultural issues—boundaries, power, and relationships in various phases of group development. Group development theory implies that the group changes and develops over time for members. In our experience and from the limited literature related to group development and racial-cultural backgrounds of participants, it is evident that racial and cultural factors play an important role in group development. Thus, the phases of the group need to be examined in terms of some of the member differences such as race and culture and of course the other social identities that surface around differences in groups and organizations. It is suggested by some that racially mixed groups, when members are polarized around stereotypic biased beliefs, can get stuck (Shaw & Barrett-Power, 1998) unless some of the members are open to exploring and working with differences. This suggests that those conducting groups should be aware of member attitudes and experiences and make attempts to work consistently with members to explore and facilitate their openness to working with difference.

QUESTIONS FOR REVIEW AND DISCUSSION

1. Identify three models of group development.

2. What are the racial and cultural issues that need to be addressed in groups as they relate to group development?

3. Write three sentences describing central points that you have drawn from reading this chapter. Try not to look back in the text—just list them from what you can recall.

4. Based on what you have read, which aspect of group development is most interesting to you? Why?

KEY TERMS AND CONCEPTS

Boundaries
Cyclical models
Models of group development
Nonsequential models
Power

Progressive models
Racial and cultural issues in groups
Relationships
Termination in groups

5

Group Dynamics in Racially and Culturally Mixed Groups

In this chapter, we explore racial and cultural dynamics in groups and organizations from a psychoanalytic and systems theory perspective to understand the psychological functioning of groups as systemic units operating in the context of a larger system. The psychoanalytic conceptual framework involves both the conscious and the unconscious processes that often surface in the form of emotional defenses against feelings of anxiety. The systemic approach involves an exploration of contextual factors, interrelatedness, and levels of functioning of subsystems that are a part of the whole. We will introduce the work of Wilfred Bion (1961) on basic assumption functioning in groups and explore the dynamics that can occur between various racial-cultural groups using examples from different groups.

Psychoanalytic Concepts

The central psychoanalytic concepts that are drawn on in understanding unconscious functioning in groups according to group relations theory are splitting, projection, and projective identification. These are concepts drawn from the work of Melanie Klein, an object relations theorist, to describe defense mechanisms that individuals use in interpersonal relationships and in groups to alleviate feelings of overwhelming anxiety. According to object relations theory, individuals are viewed as objects with which one has real and fantasized interpersonal relationships; intense feelings and desires are projected onto the objects, which serve to decrease feelings of anxiety.

SPLITTING

Splitting is the process of dividing the individuals and groups into polarized entities of good or bad; specific qualities are perceived as being contained in one and their opposites in another individual or group. At the interpersonal level, individuals split off the bad parts of themselves (onto others) to manage the anxiety associated with unacceptable aspects of the self (Wells, 1990). Splitting functions in its most negative form to rid the self of anxiety related to shameful, negative aspects of self.

At the group level, splitting involves creating polarities of good or bad, where group members perceive each other as possessing opposing qualities. Smith and Berg (1987) identify ethnocentrism, the tendency to look at the world from the perspective of one's own culture as an aspect of splitting and characterize it as a "we-they" process (p. 77). They state that this aspect of splitting is most evident during episodes of intergroup conflict in which each group views itself as good and other groups as bad, thus adhering to the conviction that the conflict will end only when the "other/bad" group is eliminated. The behavior of each group is characteristic of self-righteousness and denial of all aspects of complexity and validity between groups. In the United States, and in other countries that have been subject to colonization and domination, splitting at the intergroup level into categories of good and bad has resulted in conflict among groups that are characterized by skin color, access to power and privilege, levels of social class and education, as well as religious affiliation. Historically, these conflicts have created persecution, enslavement, genocide, and wars that have caused trauma and the loss of lives (see Figure 5.1).

PROJECTION

Projection involves projecting onto other individuals or groups one's own unacceptable desires and impulses (Kernberg, 1976). As with splitting, the quality of projection related to race and culture within groups is intricately tied to societal attitudes, expectations, prejudices, and stereotypes in both historical and contemporary contexts (Dalal, 2002). Projections related to race and culture within groups with diverse compositions also tend to be dichotomous and simplistic and, thus, reflective of societal influences related to the maintenance of power and privilege. Within a group, especially during the early stages of group development, individuals of color may receive projections related to racist stereotypical assumptions and fantasies about race. Projections concerning leadership, power, and authority may also be placed on individuals who physically represent (e.g., via skin color, gender, and language fluency) the groups with more power in society.

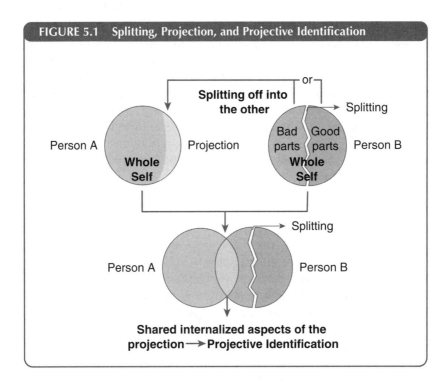

FIGURE 5.1   Splitting, Projection, and Projective Identification

The projective process, when related to race and culture, can occur irrespective of individual group members' internalized identities and valences (tendency to take up a given role). For example, in a study group that one of the authors (E.L.S.) of this text consulted several years ago, the group members, after several sessions, expressed intense dissatisfaction with the group's task of studying its own behavior in the here and now by rebelling against a perceived directive of the consultant to sit in chairs in a circle that were set up prior to their entering. The group unconsciously "chose" a young Asian woman with a valence for taking a leadership role; she declared that she no longer wished to sit in a chair, and she then sat on the floor and encouraged the other group members to sit on the floor with her. The group members complied with the young woman's request. In making this request, the young Asian woman took a leadership stance, and the group members authorized and accepted her leadership by joining her in sitting on the floor. During a later session, a discussion ensued among the members regarding who had originally suggested sitting on the floor, and the idea was attributed to a young white male (e.g., he was identified as having been the leader). This male member spoke up and denied having made the suggestion; the group then recalled that it had been the Asian female member who had taken up this leadership role. In this scenario, projections of leadership by the group were placed not on the actual member who took up a leadership role (e.g., an Asian woman, who, in some cultural contexts, based on projections about power and privilege, might not be viewed as a leader) but on a group member who, in many cultural contexts, again based on projections about power and privilege, would more often be viewed as a leader: a white male. The young white man, however, did not identify with the groups' projection, and his rejection of the projection caused the group to ultimately correctly identify the member who had taken up the leadership role.

PROJECTIVE IDENTIFICATION

Projective identification is an interactive process in which individuals and groups project undesirable or ambivalently held aspects of the self and/or group onto other individuals or groups. The individuals or groups receiving these projections identify with or may have already internalized the projections and, unconsciously, may begin to engage in behaviors that are consistent with the projections on behalf of those who projected them. The individuals or groups that are chosen to receive and internalize the projections usually have an unconscious disposition or valence for such expression (Reed & Noumair, 2000). Thus, projective identification is an unconscious defense mechanism in which the interrelatedness of individuals and/or subgroups is salient; what is projected must be salient for both parties. Moreover, there must be a connection to the projected material for both individuals and/or groups.

Projective identification may occur at the interpersonal level, for example, a spouse who is engaged in an extramarital affair, may, because of feelings of guilt and shame and the anxiety caused by these feelings, begin to fear that her or his spouse may also be behaving similarly. The guilty spouse will then become suspicious and may accuse her or his partner of being unfaithful, thus projecting her or his unwanted feelings onto the partner. The innocent spouse may deny the accusations but may also feel anger, confusion, and hurt in reaction to the spouse's accusations; these feelings are indicative of having internalized the projection. One may begin to behave differently within the relationship, for example, disconnecting from one's partner emotionally, possibly even engaging in an extramarital affair. The connection to the projected material for both partners is related to their relationship and their mutual desire for trust, intimacy, and the fear of losing the relationship. (See Figure 5.1.)

At the group level, projective identification may occur in connection with racial-cultural dynamics among individual members. Projective identification occurring in a racial-cultural context at the group level is often a microcosm of what occurs in society. For example, at the societal level, subgroups that may have greater access to power and privilege may seek to maintain status by disowning undesirable and ambivalently held aspects of themselves by projecting negative attributes onto other subgroups. Subgroups that possess attributes representative of societal stigmas related to race and culture are often the recipients of stereotyped, racist, discriminatory projections. Individuals from disenfranchised groups have, at times, in reaction to contextual dynamics, such as discrimination and oppression that perpetuates the internalization of the negative projections, enacted behaviors that are in keeping with the projections. If the young white man in the group scenario presented earlier in the chapter perceived himself as someone who needed to be the leader, because of his valence and internalized racial and gendered identities, he may have unconsciously identified with the groups' projection of him as a leader. Moreover, the Asian woman may have been offended by the lack of acknowledgment of her leadership role but may have remained silent, consciously, out of deference to the collective attitudes of the group, as well as possibly, unconsciously, conforming to Western stereotyping of Asian women as passive and nonconfrontational. Projective identification can also occur within racial-cultural groups, wherein individuals who have internalized undesirable, prejudicial attitudes from the dominant culture project them onto individuals within their own racial-cultural group. For example, African Americans can discriminate against each other on the basis of skin color differences and/or social class and educational levels. Latino Americans, Asian Americans, or Europeans can discriminate against each other on the basis of ethnicity, skin color, religion, and levels of acculturation and assimilation, as they relate, for instance, to English language fluency and levels of education and social class.

Systems Approach

A system is a "structure composed of a whole and its parts" (MacKenzie, 1990, p. 33). A group is a complex system consisting of a whole group and subgroups depending on the multiple identities of the members and their salience to the functioning of the group. Groups can have permeable and impermeable boundaries. When individuals enter groups, they are transformed because their behavior is often influenced by the group. In other words, groups can have a very powerful influence on how individuals behave. Moreover, groups are influenced by their members, and each group is different depending on its membership, leadership, and authority structure. The concept of BART is drawn from systems theory and provides the structure on which the group is created and maintained to ensure survival: *Boundaries* are psychological as well as physical and incorporate time, task, role, and territory in a group or organization (Hayden & Molenkamp, 2004). *Authority* is the right to perform work. Authority can be derived from above, meaning from those who are at higher levels within an organizational hierarchy (formal); from below, by subordinates or colleagues (informal/formal); or from within, which is an individual's capacity to take up her or his own authority (formal, informal, personal) (Obholzer, 1994). Every group or organization has an authority structure. *Role* is what defines individual activity and function in the group or organization. *Task* is the work that the group or organization is supposed to be doing or is paid to accomplish or deliver. Most groups have permeable boundaries, so that members as well as information are able to enter into the system.

Wells (1990) postulated that groups are multilevel systems with five levels of group processes: (1) intrapersonal processes, which focus on the internal life of the individual, such as personality characteristics, character structure, levels of self-awareness, and object representation; (2) interpersonal processes, which focus on relations and dynamics between individuals in a group context; (3) group-as-a-whole processes, which focus on the group's behavior as a social system and an entity as well as group members' relatedness to that system; (4) intergroup processes, which focus on relations and dynamics between and among groups in an overall system; and (5) interorganizational processes, which focus on the relationships between organizations, environmental conditions in which the organizations exist, and the impact of the environment on them. This perspective offered by Wells provides a schema for examining group and organizational processes and for diagnosing psychosocial activities and behavior.

Alderfer's (1997) theory of embedded intergroup relations further illuminates Wells's (1985) theories about intergroup-level functioning and is particularly helpful in understanding racial and cultural differences that exist within and between groups in group and organizational settings. Alderfer (1997) defines *embedded intergroup relations* as being a state of group dynamics in which neither the self nor others are free from the effects of group and intergroup dynamics on human relationships. Thus, an individual's control of intergroup dynamics can be limited; one cannot leave one's web of group affiliations, even if one wants to. Alderfer further states that every transaction between two or more people depends on the unique personalities of the individuals and the messages that individuals receive and internalize from their own group. These internalized messages are characterized by the present and historical relationships between groups that certain individuals represent.

Embedded intergroup relations theory is reflected in the racial-cultural dynamics that surface at the various levels of group processes described by Wells (1985). At the intrapersonal level, individual behavior in groups is related to an individual's racial-cultural identity, affiliation, and the impact these variables have on the group member. For example, at formation, an individual will enter the group with multiple racial-cultural and subgroup affiliations (race, culture, gender, age, religion, social class, sexual orientation, ability/disability as well as social, professional, or occupational affiliations). At the interpersonal level, individual group members may view each other as racial-cultural beings and face challenges related to internalized/externalized identities, perceptions, and projections of power, authority, and privilege (McRae, 1994). At the group level, the unit of analysis of the group and individuals are considered as interdependent subsystems, and their actions or behaviors are on behalf of the group or certain members of the group. In other words, each person is "a vehicle through which the group expresses its life" (Wells, 1990, p. 54). For example, in a large group session during a group relations conference, a black woman who expressed her anger and frustration with the group was stereotypically perceived by the group as the holder of anger; it was her valence to identify with those projections and to express them on behalf of the group (McRae et al., 2007). The black woman's unconscious valence to contain the anger of the white women as well as the other women of color made it more difficult for others to see and identify with her more vulnerable feelings, which resulted in her feeling alone with her anger. When, with the help of the consultants' interventions, the other women spoke about their anger, then the black woman was able to speak about her feelings of being alone and to express how liberating it felt to know that others had similar feelings.

The final level of Wells's (1985) multilevel system theory is interorganizational, which includes racial-cultural and subgroup affiliations as well as an individual's organizational affiliation and its impact on their interactions. Organizations have cultural dynamics; according to Carter (2000), organizational culture is often expressed through shared assumptions that are reflected in the organization's reward systems, rules, and procedures that impact performance and effectiveness. Moreover, organizations and institutions use symbolic representations that reflect company norms, cultural values, beliefs, assumptions, and other feelings related to aspects of creating positive and negative environments. For example, many organizations in the United States are embedded in dominant cultural patterns of society, which have at their core white Anglo-Saxon Protestant ideas, values, and beliefs that originated from descendants of white European ethnic groups in the United States (see Table 5.1).

TABLE 5.1 Wells's Six Levels of Organizational Process

Level of Group Functioning	Group Process	Assumptions About Group Behavior	Assumptions About Racial-Cultural Group Dynamics	Assessment of Group Behavior in a Racial-Cultural Context
Intrapersonal	Focus is on the individual and how he or she sees and relates to self; related to personality characteristics, character structure, and object representation.	Individual behavior in groups is related to personality, character, and the internal life/personal dynamics of the group member.	Individual behavior in groups is related to an individual's racial-cultural identity, affiliation, and the impact these variables have on the group member.	Individuals will behave as separate entities within the group, focusing on their personal dynamics. Racial-cultural differences and similarities will be noted but may not be openly acknowledged.
Interpersonal	Relations and dynamics between persons in a group context; the type and quality of member interactions are highlighted.	Individuals are viewed as social beings with diverse social styles and orientations.	Individuals are viewed as racial-cultural beings, and challenges arise related to internal/external identity and perceptions and projections of power, authority, and privilege.	Awareness of the pull of the group toward membership will be heightened. Projective processes related to power, authority, and privilege may occur based on external visual markers of racial and cultural affiliation.
Group-as-a-whole	The group's behavior as a social system and members' relatedness to that system.	Individual identity moves toward group identity. Tension about desires to detach and fears of engulfment will be heightened.	Individuals are viewed as containers (human vessels) as their containment function affects group identity and survival, systemically. The group becomes the container for its members.	Containment will be strongly affected by personal valence and racial-cultural/subgroup affiliation. Societal stereotyping and dominant-culture-internalized controlling images inform behavior.

Level of Group Functioning	Group Process	Assumptions About Group Behavior	Assumptions About Racial-Cultural Group Dynamics	Assessment of Group Behavior in a Racial-Cultural Context
Intergroup level	Relations and dynamics between and among groups within a system.	Groups' identity will be manifested regarding boundaries, power differences, affective patterns, cognitive formations/distortions, leadership behavior (Aldefer, 1988; EIRT).	Groups will begin to manifest political uses of racial-cultural identity related to access to institutional/systemic resources (Reed & Noumair, 2000).	Intergroup conflicts among racial-cultural identity groups may emerge; assessment of which groups are most deserving of access to institutional/systemic resources will be ongoing (Reed & Noumair, 2000).
Interorganizational level	Relationships within the organization and environmental conditions that affect it and other organizations.	Racial-cultural, subgroup, and organizational affiliations will become merged.	Groups will begin to explore/assess organizational cultural dynamics via norms, values, beliefs, assumptions, and their impact on the creation of positive or negative environments (Carter, 2000).	Groups will develop patterns of adherence to and/or differentiation from existing organizational culture (overtly and covertly).
Group-as-mother (GAM)	Group members will identify the group as a gendered object that is female and powerful (Rosenbaum, 2004).	Group members will face challenges with fusing/joining, separation, nurturance/frustration, love/hate, engulfment/estrangement, as does the infant/child with its mother (Wells, 1985).	Fantasies about racial-cultural and gendered identities and maternal role may facilitate group dynamics regarding nurturance and power or frustration/fear of power. Leadership, gender, race, and culture will be linked (Dumas, 1985).	Female group members may identify and ally with the group; male members may struggle with identification and fear of engulfment/alienation. Racial-cultural identities of the leader and members will provide a foundation for these struggles (Rosenbaum, 2004).

SOURCE: Adapted from Wells, L., Jr. (1985). The Group-as-a-Whole Perspective and Its Theoretical Roots. In A. D. Colman & M. H. Geller (Eds.), *Group Relations Reader 2* (pp. 111–113). Jupiter, FL: A.K. Rice Institute.

GROUP RELATIONS THEORY

The basic premise of group relations theory is that the group is an entity—a system whose primary task is survival. Survival as a motivating force for the group is considered to be primarily an unconscious process that occurs in any group where the members come together for a given purpose (Hayden & Molenkamp, 2004). The focus is on the group more than the individual; individual behavior is examined as occurring on behalf of and in the context of the group-as-a-whole. Thus, the individual is considered an integral part of the group-as-a-whole and is understood in the context and activities of the group. Bion (1961) hypothesized that each group member is either afraid of being engulfed by or excluded from the group. Bion's interest in group processes was initially stimulated during World War II, in his work with psychiatric patients from a rehabilitation unit. It was during this time that he noticed that the mental health of the patients seemed to be determined in large part by contextual factors related to group dynamics at both the institutional and societal levels (Rioch, 1975).

Bion (1975) considered groups to be an aggregate of individuals with a function that operated in the context of a community and society. Wells (1985) described the group-as-a-whole in holistic terms; individuals are "human vessels that reflect and express the group's gestalt" (p. 114). The concept of group-as-mother has been used as a way of describing group members' unconscious identification with the group as an ambivalently held mothering object (Wells, 1990). Wells hypothesized that the individuals' relationship to the group is similar to that of an infant with its mother. Thus, similar dynamics are experienced by group members relating to struggles with fusing/joining and separation, experiences of being nurtured/frustrated, as well as experiences with feelings of love/hate and fears of engulfment/estrangement. Rosenbaum (2004) expanded on this perspective of the group-as-mother by identifying the group as a gendered object that could be perceived, unconsciously, as female and powerful to group members. Dumas (1985) in her chapter on the dilemmas of black females in leadership discussed the challenges faced by black women in leadership roles and the expectations that organizations have of them to conform to a mythical stereotypical image as a nurturer who exists only to fulfill the social and emotional needs of individuals, as opposed to fulfilling the professional tasks and duties required of a leader within an organization. These points are particularly relevant for women who take up leadership roles in groups.

According to Bion (1961), groups function at two levels: as a work group and as a basic assumption group. In the work group, members work to accomplish a specific task in a deliberate and organized manner with a structure for meeting its objectives (Rioch, 1975). The work group is highly functional; each member has a contributing role to achieve a task in a given time period. In the work group, members usually have a clear conceptualization of the function of their roles and work to obtain appropriate information and strategies to achieve the group's goals. Although individuals in the work group may have hidden agendas or motivations, the level of functioning is one in which "members consciously pursue an agreed upon objective and deliberately engage in the completion of a work task" (Hayden & Molenkamp, 2004, p. 141). However, most groups do not always function at an optimal level; dynamics of an emotional nature occur, which may obstruct, divert, and impede group functioning. Bion (1961) called these dynamics *basic assumption functioning*. Basic assumption (ba) group functioning is usually unconscious and was initially described as consisting of three types: (1) *Basic assumption dependency* (baD) is a feeling of group dependency on the leader for knowledge and/or power. In this mode, the group will act is if it has no knowledge of the task and look to the group leader for all information and assistance. (2) *Basic assumption fight/flight* (baF/F) is characterized by a group's need to run away from authority or destroy it. In this mode, the task will be avoided or rebelled against at all costs. (3) *Basic assumption pairing* (baP) is a symbolic pairing based on the group's desire for symbolic reproduction between two individuals that will produce, in fantasy, a Savior or Messiah who will relieve the group's anxiety. Pairing between members may be represented by a positive union or an adversarial one. Two paired individuals may behave in a friendly, cooperative, and even affectionate manner, or they may be argumentative and express interpersonal conflict within the group (Lawrence et al., 1996; Rioch, 1975). Pairing can occur with members of the same or different genders.

Turquet (as cited in Lawrence et al., 1996) added *basic assumption oneness* (baO), which is characterized as a defense against differentiation and is expressed by passive participation and fusion with an omnipotent source of power, usually in the form of a designated group leader (Lawrence et al., 1996). The most recent addition is "the fifth basic assumption," basic assumption "me-ness" (baM), defined as the opposite of baO and characterized by a type of withdrawal from and denial of the group via a focus on the self (Lawrence et al., 1996, p. 143). In baM, individuals experience a fear of engulfment by the group and behave in ways that deny the reality of the group (Hayden & Molenkamp, 2004). Overall, group members' participation in basic assumption activity involves functioning as if something is true in the group. Basic assumption functioning requires very little effort; Bion (1975) stated that "participation in basic assumption activity requires no training, experience, or mental development. It is instantaneous, inevitable and instinctive" (p. 18). Basic assumption group functioning is not a negative phenomenon in groups; on the contrary, it is adaptive (e.g., because it defends against anxiety) and serves a purpose related to the group's survival.

RACIAL AND CULTURAL DYNAMICS AND GROUP RELATIONS THEORY

In diverse groups, racial and cultural dynamics are an integral part of basic assumption group functioning. Group membership can create strong feelings of anxiety among members; ba functioning is a defense mechanism that helps members cope with the anxiety they experience in the group. For example, group anxiety can be related to unarticulated issues regarding race, gender, and other cultural dynamics. Unconscious processes related to racial-cultural dynamics (e.g., the existence of stereotypes, racist/sexist/homophobic and other prejudicial attitudes) may be expressed and/or enacted by group members. For example, a group that is experiencing baD will, as previously outlined, focus on getting knowledge and power from the designated or chosen leader. However, group members experiencing baD will also be superficially aware of physical-visual differences, for example, gender, skin color, body size, and may feel anxious about being in a group where they may need to share intimate thoughts with someone very different from themselves. To decrease their anxiety, the members will act as if all members are the same and will deny and/or ignore any attempts by the leader or other members to acknowledge racial-cultural differences. Anxiety related to racial-cultural differences may, therefore, elevate their dependency needs and their baD behaviors. A group that is experiencing baF/F, in its desire to avoid anxiety by rebelling against the task or goal of the group, may choose an "alternative" leader who has physical characteristics that symbolically represent their fantasies about leadership; for example, if the leader is black, the group may unconsciously select an alternative leader among the members who is white and male or female. However, inevitably, the chosen leader will not be capable of fulfilling the group's goal of rebelling from the task, and he or she will be punished by the group (via verbal attacks, criticism, and other forms of scapegoating), and another leader will eventually emerge. Group members' interactions in baF/F may reflect superficial awareness of racial-cultural differences, but the focus will be on fighting and/or fleeing from the task. The example previously provided in this chapter of the Asian woman leading the group to sit on the floor was an attempt to take flight from the task of the group, and to join in a more informal way, in an attempt to decrease the anxiety of the authority structure that had provided the members with chairs. The group followed the young woman's leadership but later denied her leadership role.

For a group that is in the throes of baP behavior, cultural variables such as gender and race may become salient depending on the composition of the group members who are paired and the group's reaction to the pairing behavior. The pairing may also reflect some cultural aspects of the group leader as well as the system in which the group exists. For example, if two women are paired as coleaders of a group, the group may unconsciously choose two male members as an alternative to female leadership in the group. If two black people are coleaders, the group may also unconsciously choose two white members to lead. This is an example of splitting behavior by the group. When the leader points out these dynamics, the group may become anxious and defensive and may deny having any knowledge of what the leader is talking about. Despite their denials, the group members will focus solely on the paired members, unconsciously behaving as if the group has met to focus only on these two members. The group will also behave as if the two members' pairing can help the group achieve its goal. As previously stated, the interactions of the paired members may be harmonious or adversarial. As a result of their focus on the paired members, group members who are not paired may experience feelings of envy and anxiety about the pairing; these feelings will be specifically related to their fears about acceptance or rejection (e.g., pairings usually evoke longing for connection).

Members may also fantasize about the pairing related to race, gender, and culture. In a small study group consulted by the second author (E.L.S.) in the context of a graduate-level group course, the pairing of herself, an African American female, and her colleague, a white Jewish American female, evoked reactions from the group members, who eventually, unconsciously, chose two white gay males, who were intimately involved, as informal leaders of the group. These two male members often shared personal stories about their relationship with members outside the group and were ultimately set up by the group to sabotage the group's work during the sessions conducted in the class. Thus, the pair succeeded in leading the group outside the boundaries of the class, perpetuating the "as if" fantasy that the group could only work outside the boundary of the formal group. Splitting also occurred regarding the coconsultants' racial-cultural identities based on the group's fantasies; as a black woman, the second author (E.L.S.) was perceived as having more authority (because of her racial and gendered similarity to the African American female professor) and as being angrier and more critical, while the white Jewish American coconsultant was perceived as being more nurturing, patient, and personable by the mostly white group members (Short, 2007).

A group that is following the leadership of one individual, as in baO, will resist focusing on differentiation at a variety of levels; however, the race and culture of the "omnipotent" leader may overtly or covertly affect the group dynamic. For example, if the leader is a person of color, individuals of color within that group may be perceived as having more power and privilege than white group members. Or if the leader is a female, females in the group may be perceived as being powerful. An example of this is a small study group at a group relations conference in which African American, Afro-Caribbean, Latina, Asian, and other female members of color experienced having more power and privilege to explore racial-cultural and gendered dynamics related to authority and leadership due to the fact that the conference director was an African American woman. Other examples of this phenomenon as it relates to racial-cultural aspects of baO can be seen throughout history, for example, with religious cults, enslavement, domination, oppression of one group over another, and with group identification with the oppressor (see Table 5.2).

Table 5.2 Basic Assumption Group Process

Basic Assumption	Group Process	Assumptions About Group Behavior	Assumptions About Racial-Cultural Group Dynamics	Assessment of Group Behavior in a Racial-Cultural Context
Basic assumption dependency (baD) (Bion, 1961)	The group has a dependency on the leader to get knowledge/power.	The group members will behave as if they have no knowledge of the task and will look to the leader to provide it.	The group members may suppress the salience of racial-cultural differences due to high levels of anxiety.	Group members will act "as if" all members are the same and will deny and/or ignore any attempt by the leader or members to acknowledge racial-cultural differences.
Basic assumption fight/flight (baF/F) (Bion, 1961)	The group will express a need to fight/flee from the task and will ignore/rebel against the designated leader.	The group members will acknowledge an awareness of the task but will avoid, ignore, and denigrate the task.	The group members may choose an "alternative" leader who may have physical characteristics that represent their fantasies of leadership.	Group members' interactions may reflect superficial awareness of racial-cultural differences, but group focus will be on fighting or fleeing from the task.
Basic assumption pairing (baP) (Bion, 1961)	The group will focus on a pairing that will "save" them from the task.	The group members will ignore/avoid the task in favor of focusing on the pairing.	The choice of paired members may reflect the racial-cultural composition of the group and/or the leader, but conscious awareness of this will be limited.	Group members will focus solely on the paired group members. Interactions of the paired members can be positive or adversarial. Group members may also experience feelings of envy and anxiety about acceptance or rejection in relation to the paired members. They may also fantasize about the pairing related to race, gender, and culture.

Basic Assumption	Group Process	Assumptions About Group Behavior	Assumptions About Racial-Cultural Group Dynamics	Assessment of Group Behavior in a Racial-Cultural Context
Basic assumption oneness (baO) (Turquet, as cited in Hayden & Molenkamp, 2004).	The group members will become dependent on an "omnipotent" leader who will "save" them from the anxiety of the task.	The group members will be passive and dependent in service of a focus on the leader.	Differentiation of race and culture will be denied and avoided. Racial-cultural characteristics of the chosen leader will be processed unconsciously.	Group members who reflect the racial-cultural characteristics of the chosen leader may have more power and privilege and enact behavior that reflects their dominance.
Basic assumption me-ness (baM) (Lawrence et al., 1996).	Group members will deny and/or detach from the group and task in favor of reliance on the self. Group members may form pairings and subgroups outside formal group boundaries.	Group members will view the group and the task as a threat to their individuality.	Individuality may be expressed in a racial-cultural context. Detachment from the group and reliance on the self may be adaptive on to manage anxiety related to fears of engulfment and rejection (Short, 2007).	Group members may engage in parasitic attaching outside the group to others who are similar or different, racially and culturally. Group members will not, however, share their learning from these attachments with the group-as-a-whole (Short, 2007).

SOURCE: Adapted from Wells, L., Jr. (1985). The Group-as-a-Whole Perspective and Its Theoretical Roots. In A. D. Colman & M. H. Geller (Eds.), *Group Relations Reader 2* (pp. 111–113). Jupiter, FL: A.K. Rice Institute.

Group-level baM, in which members may withdraw from and deny the reality of the group in favor of a focus on the self, may, in addition to being related to a fear of engulfment by the group (Hayden & Molenkamp, 2004), also be related to the need to manage cultural, personal boundaries of race, gender, sexual orientation, age, role, and valence. Excessive focus on the management of these types of boundaries may lead group members to engage in acts of parasitic attachment to group members who are similar or different from them racially and culturally, resulting in pairings or subgroups that connect outside the formal group boundaries. Learning will occur from these attachments, but group members will not share what they have learned or experienced with the group-as-a-whole (Short, 2007). Research on the impact of race and culture on group dynamics has found evidence that physiological distress among participants involved in interracial intergroup interactions/ activities can lead individuals to detach and turn inward, thus creating an isolative state (Mendes et al., 2002, as cited in Goode, 2007). Thus, baM group behavior may be adaptive and not pathological, characterized as an act of dependency on the self, and related to issues of survival of the psyche (Short, 2007) (see Table 5.2).

We have found the five primary characteristics of embedded intergroup relations theory to be very helpful in understanding racial-cultural dynamics that occur in groups and systems (Alderfer & Smith, 1982): (1) group boundaries, (2) power differences, (3) affective patterns, (4) cognitive formations and distortions, and (5) leadership behavior. Group boundaries, which can be physical and psychological, determine and influence membership and characterize permeability as it relates to other groups. Group boundaries serve as a "metaphoric container of anxieties carried by individual members as a consequence of their group membership" (Berg & Smith, 1990, p. 116). The concept of containment in groups implies that the group can be held as a safe enough container for members to engage in. Containment refers to boundaries of the group as well as an emotional sense of safety for members. Power differences at the intergroup level often involve issues of availability and control of resources. Power is intricately tied to access to resources and assumptions about the scarcity of them systemically. Thus, questions about which group will have access to and is deserving of those limited, systemic resources may be related to what Reed and Noumair (2000) describe as *political uses* of racial-cultural identity at intergroup levels:

> Within institutional settings, questions of diversity are frequently raised in relation to the allocation of resources—programs, positions, time, funding, and so on. If a group is perceived as systematically disadvantaged, then a case can be made that this group is deserving of proportionately greater institutional resources. There may be significant intergroup conflict related to which groups are most deserving of corrective advantage. Identity groups and individuals

may minimize their own advantage or emphasize their disadvantage within the context of such discussions. We refer to this as the relationship between context and currency: What chips are worth the most in what context, and how is public identity selected and displayed to others on this basis? (pp. 62–63)

Reed and Noumair's (2000) description of the political uses of intergroup racial-cultural identity is also connected to the fourth (intergroup) level characteristic: affective patterns of embedded intergroup relations. Affective relational patterns include positive and negative feelings among members about those who are perceived as being in and out of the group. Cognitive formations are formed and conditioned by each group's boundaries, power differences, and affective patterns, as well as the contextual, systemic impact, objectively and subjectively, of relations between groups. If racial-cultural identification is an integral component of a group's boundaries, systemically, cognitive formations will reflect this dynamic. For example, the phenomenon of victimization is a source of identity for some disenfranchised groups. The emotional connections and unification caused by their experiences with oppression may increase group cohesion. In a study of small study groups in group relations conferences, it was found that when Latinos, gays and lesbians, African Americans, and Asians were a majority in the groups they were in, they felt more powerful than in groups where they were a minority (McRae, Orbe, Patel, & Hsu, 2008). When they were at least half the total number in the group, they often took leadership and controlled the topic of group discussions. The final characteristic—leadership behavior—is related to each group's representative, their behavior in a systemic context, and how that behavior is reflective of the group's permeability (Alderfer & Smith, 1982). In racially and culturally diverse groups, it is important to pay attention to who takes up leadership and how the role is related to the existing authority structure. In uncovering salient characteristics of leadership behavior systemically, it is important to (a) find out whether the chosen leader is a reflection of the membership in terms of racial or cultural representation or other factors, (b) identify the groups' process of choosing a leader, (c) identify how the leader is authorized to take up the leadership role, and (d) identify whether the leader has the authority to autonomously make decisions on behalf of the group or whether he or she is merely a figurehead who is made use of by the group and is not fully authorized to make decisions for the group-as-a-whole.

Case Example

We use a case example to demonstrate how some of the concepts discussed above are enacted in group life. The vignette is drawn from a small study group in a group relations conference with the theme of working with differences: "The Complexity of Color and Culture in Group and Organizational

Life." In this conference, we formed small study groups based on how members self-identified on the registration application. The group described here was playfully identified by the research team as the "Rainbow Group," because they had such a diverse mixture of members in comparison with other groups that were all white, all people of color, half Latino, and so on. This group displayed a number of basic assumption behaviors that can be related to issues of power, affect, cognitions, and leadership.

In this group, there were three Asian, three black, one Latino, and five white people. An African American woman consulted the members of this racially diverse small group. The session began with a discussion between two black women and one black male (who self-identified as gay) and focused on the question of whether or not one is powerful when one speaks in conference events. The discussion of power, led by these three members, continued for some time without verbal recognition of color and culture or without reference by the consultant or the members to the power and authority this trio was clearly exercising in leading the group discussion. The discussion flowed into a conversation between two paired members—a young white male and the black male about privilege, with the white male denying his privilege and the black male politely challenging the white male's denial. A young black female interrupted their discussion and addressed the issue of color, asking the group why it hadn't "come up" in any of the small group sessions. None of the group members responded to her question, so she began, with the assistance of a young Asian woman, to interview the two males who had been speaking, asking them how they felt about engaging in a discussion of privilege with each other. Their responses continued in the same vein as before. In this group, the men talked about power and privilege and the women attempted to engage them about race. Several women spoke openly about race; the young black woman challenged the group to "go deeper" concerning their dialogues about racial issues, and she was joined by a young white woman who validated and agreed with her challenge. The black male joined the females regarding the importance of taking up their authority in the group to speak about race and culture. A young Asian female, who had been less talkative, spoke about the difficulty she frequently experienced in taking up a leadership role to talk about race and culture in groups.

Toward the end of the session, the female consultant made several interventions that aroused the group members; one consultation related to the complexity of understanding race and culture. She stated that the group had "sandwiched" her, an African American woman, between two white males and inquired about the meaning of this; she referred to herself as a black woman who "sounds white," and, finally, she challenged the stereotype of the silent Asian female by pointing out that the Asian female member was the first member to speak at the start of the session. The consultant's comment about the white males caused an immediate denial by the males in question; her other interventions about complexity were also ignored, but her comment about stereotypes was validated by the young black woman who had earlier in the session challenged the group to work less superficially. She shared with the group that she felt silenced and invisible at her job.

Initially, this group had strong feelings of dependency (baD) on the consultant and was often angry at her for not answering all their questions and for not engaging with them like a member. One of the challenges for consultants in small study groups at group relations conferences is the very seductive pull to abandon the leadership role and become a member. In this group, the members responded to the consultant's refusal to abandon her leadership role by ignoring her interventions. Whenever the group behaved in this way, the consultant would verbally observe that her interventions were being ignored, which served to illuminate the group's behavior in relation to her role. The task of the group was to study its own behavior in the here and now of the experience. Their behavior of ignoring the consultant's interventions was unconscious and indicative of the group's relationship to power, authority, and role. Thus, although they could talk about power, privilege, and racial-cultural factors having a role in their interactions, it was too frightening for them to explore what that role was and how it was taking shape in the group in the here and now. One way of taking flight from the anxiety of the here and now is to talk *about* a topic instead of *reacting to it,* such as touching the dirt but not wanting to get your hands dirty. The group dealt with its dependency needs by choosing an alternative leader—a young black woman who asked questions and responded readily (unlike the consultant)—who represented their fantasies about leadership. This young woman, however, was very similar to the consultant in terms of race and gender. In this group, there was also behavior that was indicative of possessing the power and privilege of being black; both the consultant of the group and the director of the conference were black women. The issue of racial-cultural representation for this group and the members' feelings about it would have been an enlightening and powerful learning, but it was too frightening for them to explore. Thus, discussion of power without acknowledgment of who was assuming leadership roles in the group and what that meant dynamically denoted a flight from the designated task of being in the here and now.

baP occurred in the group when the young black female and a young Asian female took up leadership roles (covertly) by interviewing the two paired males. Each of these pairs was racially and culturally different, which suggested the groups' desire to work across differences and perhaps a fantasy that these pairs could save the group from the difficulties and challenges of exploring differences in groups. The two white males who flanked the African American female consultant represented the containment of black female authority by white males. This containment may have unconsciously served to simultaneously protect and inhibit the African American female consultant. In the vignette, the group members' covert, unconscious enactment of power, privilege, and authority as it related to race and culture was challenged by the consultant in several instances, particularly in her reference to the group's relationship to her authority and the complexity of her identity.

Summary

This chapter has introduced group relations theory as a combination of psychoanalytic and systems theory. Defense mechanisms of splitting, projection, and projective identification have been outlined. Group-as-a-whole and embedded intergroup relations theories have been outlined and explored as they relate to group functioning. Five types of basic assumption functioning have been defined and applied to group behavior. Racial and cultural dynamics are highlighted as an integral part of dynamics that occur in mixed groups. The authors have taken existing theoretical concepts and incorporated racial-cultural factors that play a role in group interactions. The case vignette and Tables 5.1 and 5.2 have been provided to illustrate how the theoretical concepts can be expanded to include racial and cultural dynamics in groups.

QUESTIONS FOR REVIEW AND DISCUSSION

1. Identify the three types of psychoanalytic defense mechanisms that groups use to avoid anxiety. Think about whether or not you have used any of them in group or interpersonal settings.

2. Describe Wells's (1990) and Alderfer's (1994) theories of multilevel group functioning.

3. Identify the five types of basic assumption group functioning. How are they affected by racial-cultural dynamics?

4. What do Reed and Noumair (2000) identify as the political uses of racial-cultural identity in groups?

KEY TERMS AND CONCEPTS

Basic assumption: dependency/fight/flight/ pairing/oneness/me-ness

Embedded intergroup relations theory

Group-as-a-whole

Group relations theory

Object relations theory

Projection

Projective identification

Splitting

6

Social Roles in Groups

Role, in groups, in organizations, and in institutional contexts, has been defined in a variety of ways. According to the *Merriam-Webster Dictionary, role* is defined as (1) "a character assigned or assumed" (such as the role of father or mother) (2) "a socially expected behavior pattern usually determined by an individual's status in a particular society" (such as an actor, teacher, athlete), and (3) "a function or part performed especially in a particular operation or process" (*Merriam-Webster Dictionary Online,* n.d). Social roles in groups and organizations are related to the character—leader, member, administrator—the social expectations of those who take up these roles, and the function that each serves on the part of the group or organization. In this chapter, we discuss social roles in racially and culturally mixed groups. We purport that there are added assumptions, perceptions, and attitudes ascribed to those who take up the various social roles in groups due to the social and cultural context in which the group takes place. Some awareness and understanding of the dynamic intersection of these factors are crucial in working with diverse groups and organizations. First, some definitions drawn from the group literature are provided, and then five types of social roles are outlined. Finally, social roles, as they relate to group-as-a-whole, role suction, and racial-cultural factors involved in role taking in groups, will be explored.

Wells (1990) stated that roles are formed based on the expectations, projections, and projective identification of the group members and are both defensive and adaptive for group life. He defined role differentiation as "the vehicle by which group members manage their conflicts, ambivalence, and tasks" (p. 67). His description is related to the expectations and symbolic meaning of the role taken. The description of taking up a role provided by Gillette and McCollom (1995) is more functional in terms of what an individual symbolizes in service to the group. Roles are characterized by differentiation that helps to manage anxiety, defend against de-individualization or estrangement, and contribute to the group's structure and process, all in service of the group's task.

Role involves an internal and external conception and an image for each group member. The role that members of the group take up is related to a number of factors that include personality, race, culture, gender, sexual orientation, and other variables. Social identity can greatly influence all of these aspects of role. Also, as defined in previous chapters, social identity encompasses racial-cultural characteristics, such as skin color, hair color/texture, ethnicity, language, gender, sexual orientation, age, and ability/disability. Social identity has multiple layers of embeddedness, and group membership is dependent on the messages that individuals receive from their own and other groups with which they are affiliated (Alderfer, 1997). Each member has multiple social identities, with one being more salient than others in a given context. Group membership is intricately connected to role, and an individual's affiliation with multiple social identity groups is related to the types of roles that they will take up in service of a group task. For example, the first role that individuals have is that of a family member; within the family group, roles are based on an individual's valence as well as the needs of the family unit. Often, in a variety of group settings, the role that a person assumes in their family of origin will be quite similar in quality and type to the roles that the individual assumes throughout their life span.

Person-in-Role

The phrase "person-in- role" is used because individual members assume roles based on personality, temperament, and basic assumption functioning. Those roles are both in service of the group task and based on their valency or their predisposition to take up certain roles (Hayden & Molenkamp, 2004). The process of taking up a role is both conscious and unconscious. As previously stated, individuals may have a familiarity with their own valence (conscious) but less awareness of the influence that the group has on them to take up certain roles in service of the survival of the group. Rioch (1985) writes about the dynamics of person-in-role:

> And so we not only have the person and the role, which always used to seem to me to be a clear kind of duality, but we also have the role created by the need of the group. We have the person and the role as perceived not only from the inside of the *person* playing the *role,* but also from the outside. What are "*they,*" the *people,* the *group* making of this *person* and this role? And do not their perceptions influence how the person perceives himself and his role? (p. 366)

In this chapter, the concept of person-in-role is broadened to encompass racial-cultural dynamics that influence internal and external perceptions of role. An individual's valence, in addition to personality and temperament, is characterized by race, culture, stereotypes, and projections that are connected to these aspects of social identity and role (McRae, 2004).

Social Roles in Groups

Each group creates social roles as a vehicle to attain its goal. These roles are formed on behalf of the group-as-a-whole. The act of taking up roles impacts the group's functioning by simultaneously illuminating existing differences and similarities among members. According to Smith and Berg (1987), this differentiation among group members has been found to embody three distinct categories: (1) dominant-submissive, (2) friendly-unfriendly, and (3) instrumentally controlled–emotionally expressive. Smith and Berg discuss the paradox of a group's need for differentiation among members in order to survive but state that differences also create conflicts that threaten its survival.

Stereotypes concerning race and culture can be linked to the categories described by Smith and Berg (1987) of group member differentiation and can influence perceptions and expectations for the group-as-a-whole. For example, as was mentioned in Chapter 3, African American women and men often receive stereotyped projections of anger and aggression (unfriendly) and emotional expressiveness. Many Asian American women and men are often stereotyped as being passive (submissive) and less talkative in the group. White males often receive stereotypes of dominance, white women are labeled submissive, and both genders are frequently stereotyped as being instrumentally controlled and not emotionally expressive. These stereotypes impact perceptions and expectations of the way a person might take up various social roles in the group and influence behaviors of the group-as-a-whole.

Social roles in groups can also influence the group-as-a-whole in an organizational and/or institutional context. For example, the existence of diversity in institutions often has socio-historical and political significance that is intricately connected to power and privilege. Power and privilege, in organizational and institutional contexts, can be defined as access to or control of material, social, and institutional resources (Reed & Noumair, 2000). Reed and Noumair cite a group conference that focused on diversity in which a white male consulted to a small study group. The authors describe a scenario in which the group members initially ignored the white male consultant. Group members expressed disappointment at being in a group consulted to by a white male at a conference focused on the theme of diversity. At some point during the conference, however, group members received information about the consultant's sexual orientation. He was gay. This information was not a secret in the conference system. However, having access to this information about the consultant resulted in a dramatic shift of the group's attitude toward him. The members began to focus exclusively on the fact that he was a gay man and ignored his race. In accordance with this shift, gay and lesbian group members were given an elevated status, which lead to the development of a powerful "gay and lesbian alliance" and, thus, a focus on the oppression of gay and lesbian individuals within the conference (pp. 65–66).

In keeping with this dynamic, as African American women in positions of authority as professors, conference directors, and/or consultants, we have also experienced similar dynamics. Race and gender, which in some contexts might engender invisibility and oppression, often create an environment (e.g., in the classroom, group settings, conferences) in which individuals of color are perceived to have an elevated status and increased access to power and privilege. The following excerpted portions of transcript are from a small study group at a conference that was directed by the first author, and consulted to by the second author. The members' comments illustrate the impact that social role and authority has on group members politically, contextually, and emotionally. The first group member, an African American woman, states,

> I'm kind of like back to the original, like, something the consultant had mentioned, about, just the issue that we have with an African American woman in leadership. I don't know. Do people have problems with that? I'm searching, and I feel, I really appreciate [that] a woman of color is actually in the role of consultant, or even, directing this whole thing, and I think it's run very smoothly. But I have to say, and it may be so much easier to look at someone else. I know you keep saying you're the scapegoat, this and that, but you're putting yourself in that role. But you have to acknowledge that you really aren't acknowledging and respecting the people who are running the show; do you know what I mean?

Another group member, an African Latina woman, describes her feelings about social identity, role, and leadership in relation to the conference director:

> I'm with the same department as her, and there's a feeling of, almost like protection. Like, oh God, I hope everything goes okay. Which is an insecurity from my own internal stuff. You know, as a black woman. You know. It must be perfect, kind of. It's doesn't really have to be at the conscious level, but unconsciously, I'm like, yes! Okay. You know, things are going well. I'm kind of rooting for her, while she doesn't really need me to do that. (Laughter) She's very competent. But, there are all those feelings that come up, to have a woman, black woman, in either, as a consultant, or as the leader, because that's not what I'm used to in society. And sometimes, it does bring up feelings that, and not necessarily that she shouldn't be there, but, other feelings. In general, because I'm colored, and because of her race, and, I feel she's representing me, and I want people to feel okay.

Finally, a third member corroborates other members' comments:

> Actually, I have two things I want to say. First, in response to what you just said, I work at a school. And, it has an office in Brooklyn Heights with a woman in power, who happens to be African American. And when you said that, we look at her we're in awe, because, like wow, she made it. And I guess, I'm not black myself, obviously, but, I feel the same way about my boss, because, a lot of times, like she must have overcome so much, like in an institution, there's like, everyone in power is usually someone white or male, and a lot of times, I just . . . I look at her, and I, I'm just amazed and I also hope someday that I can do that, because I want to be a person of power in authority some day, in the university, too.

The comments of these group members reflect a focus on social role, leadership, and authority; the members are overtly focused on these aspects as they relate to both the conference director and group consultant. They also are simultaneously and unconsciously enacting and exploring aspects of power and privilege in relation to each other in the group. In this group with predominantly black and Asian members, there was a preoccupation with issues of race, gender, leadership, and authority by black, Latina, and Asian women. Racial-cultural issues were central to the group, with issues of collectivism versus individualism, with members taking up a number of roles to attain their goals of working with the complexity of color and culture. In this example as in the first, members from disenfranchised social identity groups took up roles of leadership, power, and influence that were intricately tied to the social identity of the conference director and group consultant. In both cases racial-cultural factors and social identity of the members and leaders influenced group members' behavior.

Social Roles and Defense Mechanisms: Role Suction and Role Types

As stated earlier, social roles are a part of the group's structure. They are considered to be functional roles, such as task-oriented roles (initiator, information seeker and giver, coordinator, energizer, evaluator-critic), group-building and maintenance roles (harmonizer, tension releaser, compromiser, feeling expresser, gatekeeper), and self-centered roles (aggressor, dominator, blocker, recognition seeker) (Wilson & Hanna, 1990). Others refer to them as problematic roles (monopolizer, advice giver, socializer, intellectualizer, acting superior) of members in groups (Corey & Corey, 2006; Jacobs, Masson, & Harvill, 2002). All refer to the types of roles that members take up in the group. Our stance is similar to that of Wells (1990); role types emerge in groups as both defensive and adaptive mechanisms. The defense is against anxiety, and the adaptation is a way of delineating, isolating conflicts, containing, and providing psychological security for members.

Social roles in groups, as in society, are often characterized by the need to have an identified "other" on which to displace and project negative thoughts, feelings, and desires in service of denying and/or sublimating anxiety. This process of "othering" is expressed by enactments of defense mechanisms at a group level. The commonly used defense mechanisms in groups—splitting, projection, and projective identification—were discussed in Chapter 5. These defense mechanisms are intricately tied to the types of roles that individuals may take up in groups.

The valence or personal tendencies of an individual member, combined with the expectations and projections of other members, emerge into a particular role type that is assigned to the individual. Horowitz (1985) defined the pull of the group as *role suction,* which is characterized by group forces that act in powerful ways to unconsciously pressure a person into a needed role. Splitting, projection, and projective identification are all involved in this process; the person-in-role has a containment function for other members' projections. The person-in-role is also manipulated to engage in behaviors that are necessary for the group's survival. Horowitz stresses that tension between an individual's valence and the group's needs always exists. Moreover, the group is usually skilled at unconsciously recognizing which members have a valence for expressing certain emotions, for instance, anger, seductiveness, dependency, and dominance. Specific role types within groups also characterize the phenomenon of person-in-role in groups. Below some of the role types are discussed and then related to the racial and cultural stereotypes ascribed to members. The following descriptions are examples of types of roles that members often take up during the life of a group.

THE LEADER

Individuals who possess a valence for leadership and speaking in groups usually take up the role of leader. The leadership role may fluctuate among several group members. Horowitz (1985) identifies this role as the *spokesperson role,* in which a member takes up a leadership role in order to express dominant group themes. One of the most dominant group themes that an individual in the leadership role may express is the tension between their valence for taking up the role and the group's needs. Thus, the leader may be characterized as exhibiting more assertive and questioning behaviors. The leader may be willing to take more risks than others in the group. Often the leader is more task oriented and will initiate topics for discussion and make suggestions about what the group needs to do. For example, at the start of many small groups, individuals will introduce themselves and suggest that other members do the same. The act of making the suggestion is a move, consciously or unconsciously, toward leadership. Other member's acquiescence is indicative of followership, and the act of identifying themselves is an enactment of the group's need to differentiate and initiate joining, in order to manage existing group level anxiety.

Racial-cultural dynamics impact this role in several ways—the chosen leader may possess external, physical characteristics similar to that of the formal group leader/facilitator and those in authority positions at the institution in which the group is embedded. The leader may also have physical resemblance to societal images of leadership (e.g., male and white). For example, in a small study group where there were one Latino, Asian, and one African man, two white men, two white women, and one black woman, the two white males took up leadership in deciding what the group would discuss for the first three sessions. When the consultant pointed this out and asked the group why this happened, the members discarded the intervention, stating that it was just a coincidence. When it happened again during the next two sessions, the consultant decided to point it out as a pattern that members might learn something from. An intervention was made in which the consultant wondered what it meant that these two men were taking such responsibility for the group's focus. The consultant asked the group, "In this very diverse group who is authorized to take up leadership roles and why?" The Latino man stated he had noticed, and he thought that based on his experience, this is not unusual. He stated that he was okay with what was happening in the group because he was not letting it bother him. The African man stated that he had not really noticed it. He also stated that it was okay with him if they wanted to "try and lead the group." The Asian man stated that he worked with one of the white men and that is just the way he is, he likes to coordinate and organize people. While this dialogue was occurring, the women sat quietly, watching the men. Eventually, one of the white women stated that if this is what the group wanted, she did not see anything wrong with it. She said someone else might take up leadership in the group at another time.

The group, at this point in their development, seemed quite comfortable with the white men taking up the leadership role. However, they were uncomfortable exploring the racial-cultural issues that seemed so obvious to the consultant, who was an African American woman. The consultant, understanding the importance of timing, decided not to pursue the topic any more during that session. She hypothesized that the group might have some feelings about her leadership and felt more comfortable with white male leaders, especially in an institution where white men held most of the dominant positions. Thus, she concluded that the members seemed comfortable maintaining the status quo. The leadership role often runs parallel to and can be competitive with the role of the formal group leader/facilitator. The role (e.g., who takes it up and what it elicits at group level) should be viewed as an expression of what the group needs, developmentally, to progress and survive.

THE FOLLOWER

The group needs both leaders and followers in order to function; leadership cannot exist without followership. Thus, the two roles and the behaviors they engender are symbiotic in their relationship to each other. The role of the follower can be characterized by dependence, acceptance, silence, and support of dominant group themes and expressions. Follower behavior is often an unconscious barometer of group anxiety related to authority at multiple levels. For example, dependent and accepting behaviors are often connected to a group's need to elicit approval from an authority figure (e.g., the formal group leader/facilitator). Follower behavior can also be indicative of unconscious processes related to the developmental stages of a group—for example, the process of entering and joining at the start of the group, when members are often uncertain of what to do or how to behave with a new group of people. In the group described above, the members were tentative about being in a new group and wanted to see what others had to say. People of color, who are in a group for the first time and who have had limited or no exposure to groups or therapeutic work, may take the role of follower until they can assess the situation. It is also important to point out that in order for groups to function effectively, there must be followers who are willing to contribute to the work of the group.

Basic assumption oneness also typifies the follower role; group members become dependent on an omnipotent leader they believe will save them from the anxiety of the task. Behavior in this type of basic assumption functioning will be primarily passive and dependent (Turquet, as cited in Hayden & Molenkamp, 2004). Racial-cultural dynamics of the follower role can be connected to stereotypes and projections of leadership roles (e.g., societal expectations that certain physical characteristics equate followership). This was demonstrated in the example above, where the members from the more disenfranchised groups allowed the white men to take up leadership roles. As the group moved forward, the two white men engaged in a struggle for leadership, and the other members sat quietly, watching them argue. When the consultant asked what the two men might represent for the group, members responded to the cool intellectualism of one and the emotional expressionism of the other. They seemed more connected to the emotional man who was gay; he was described as being more like them. Their identification of him as gay, and a member of a disenfranchised group, plus the fact that he had taken classes with a few of the members, were discussed. In identifying this connection to the gay male member, it seemed that the straight white man was being isolated in his leadership role in the group.

Another cultural construct that can be connected with this role is language fluency. The formal group leader and members can silence individual members, for whom the language of the group is not their first/native language, due to the challenges with fluency, comprehension, and concerns of negative judgment. Silence of this type among members can be perceived as an embodiment of the follower role. Anxiety about one's minority status in a group (e.g., being the "only one" of a particular racial/ethnic/gendered category) can also engender enactment of the follower role. In one group, an Asian student would only speak when asked a question. One member complained that the student was too quiet and accused her of not contributing to the group. In response, the Asian student stated she did not want to disturb the group, since she had to translate what was said in her head and then form appropriate responses. She felt it would take up too much of the group's time for her to engage more actively, so she would only speak when absolutely necessary. The group leader then asked if the members could let her know when they were willing to take extra time to hear what she had to say.

THE REBEL/ALTERNATIVE LEADER

The role of the rebel can be characterized as an alternative leader of the group. This role has many of the same characteristics as the leadership role but is more overtly in competition, behaviorally, with the formal leader/facilitator role. It is often characterized by basic assumption behavior related to fighting authority or fleeing from group tasks that have been designated by the authority figure at the group, organizational, and/or institutional levels. Role suction in this context is often more fluid. A variety of members may take up the rebel role, but its dominant role behavior is always of alternative leadership that minimizes, flees from, or destroys the group task. To that end, the group responds behaviorally through in-fighting, arguing, and competing in service of avoidance of the task (Hayden & Molenkamp, 2004). The rebel role is primarily one that challenges the formal authorized leader as well as the task of the group.

Racial-cultural aspects of this role will reflect group members' projections and fantasies of the individuals who take up the rebel role. In the diverse small study group described above, the gay white male became the rebel. He got angry with the consultant for bringing up the issue of race, stating that he did not see it as an issue that needed to be discussed. He questioned the existence of unconscious processes and asked if the consultant had constructed the situation to stir things up. He also wondered how the group would be different if their consultant was of another race or gender. His comments represented the group's wish to deposit its uncomfortable feelings about race and its fears of inadequacies to manage the conflicts into the consultant. At this juncture in the group's development, it was very important for the consultant not to get defensive and to help the group explore their feelings about the consultant's authority in the group.

THE MEDIATOR

Group building and maintenance characterize the mediator role. The mediator acts as the harmonizer and works to avoid conflict among group members. The mediator role, like the leader, the follower, and rebel roles, is concerned with group survival and avoidance of anxiety through management of group behavior related to competition and emotional affect among group members. The mediator role may embody a variety of behaviors, including denial of differences among members, an overt focus on joining and pairing, and seductive behavior. Like the rebel role, the mediator role may also embody conscious or unconscious flight behavior. However, the manner in which the flight is initiated will be neutral and (overtly) nonaggressive. For example, at most group relations conferences, a primary task of the study group is for the members to struggle with being fully present with each other (e.g., being in the "here and now"). Group behavior in the here and now often necessitates direct interaction among members about their feelings for each other based on what has been said and enacted. These interactions often serve to heighten group level anxiety. Increasing levels of anxiety are often consciously and unconsciously avoided at group level. Thus, an enactment of anxiety avoidance in the mediator role is often characterized by an abrupt change of subject or shift in focus of content during a group session, which serves to move the group away from the here and now and, thus, lessen anxiety.

Another example, from the small group described above, was a white woman who often stepped in to help the group manage the struggle between the two white men. She would make statements like, "We are all members of this group and what each of us have to say is important; there is no need to take sides or to fight." Role suction, as with the leader role, is strongly impacted by the valence of the member to take up a role that is usually similar to those they hold outside of the group. Insight can occur for group members when they can make the connection between their valences, as observed in the similarity of roles they take up inside and outside of the group. Racial-cultural dynamics related to the mediator role may be associated with gender and age (e.g., the mediator role may often be taken up by a female member or an older member). It also may be associated with cultural preferences that regard overt expressions of emotion and self-disclosure as taboo in group and public contexts (Sue & Sue, 2008). The emergence and existence of the mediator role should be viewed as evidence of the group's unconscious need to develop a pattern of engaging in and detaching from conflict, and/or expressions of emotion in the here and now, in service of lessening and managing anxiety.

THE SCAPEGOAT

The scapegoat, although as integral to a group's life as the other roles outlined in this chapter, is one of the most feared and disliked roles. Like the leader, rebel, and mediator roles, the scapegoat role emerges in response to the group's need to avoid task-related anxiety and is intricately connected to issues of group survival. The unconscious processes involved in the emergence of the scapegoat are related to defense mechanisms of group displacement of unwanted feelings, thoughts, and desires onto a member who is deemed to be nonthreatening and a willing container. Projective identification is an important aspect of the emergence and maintenance of the scapegoat role. Containment of unwanted, undesirable aspects of the group's unconscious processes is the principle function of an individual who assumes this role. Miller (1974) described scapegoating as "a stereotyped example in groups where shared patterns of denial are focused by the process of projective identification on one member. That member is asked and often agrees to express all of the given undesirable attitudes for the group" (p. 12). Thus, in addition to role suction, there is an unconscious awareness of the valence of an individual to contain this type of material at both the group and individual levels.

Racial-cultural aspects of scapegoating, as with other roles, are overtly connected to societal, stereotyped representations of race and culture. Scapegoating can occur when members who take up leadership roles prove to be inadequate leaders. The act of scapegoating behavior in this instance is usually related to unconscious group-level disappointment and anger toward the formal, designated leader/facilitator. In the small study group described above with the two white male leaders, the straight white man was scapegoated. He was seen as not competent enough to lead the group and was blamed for them not doing well on a group project. His rival called him an impostor who thought he was more intelligent than the other members. He was alienated in the group. When the white woman who took up the role of mediator attempted to rescue him, he shunned her attempts by denying any responsibility for the outcome of the project. Thus, he agreed or on some level wanted to stay in the scapegoated role.

Members who are scapegoated are mistreated and can be abused by the group. The experience of being scapegoated is often quite painful and confusing. It can result in the member being ejected by the group—either by overt rejection or by the member electing to leave the group. This ejection can symbolically represent "elimination" or "killing off" a member who embodies the unwanted, negative aspects that the group wishes to deny. The short story by Shirley Jackson (1948), "The Lottery," depicts a scenario in which community members engage in an annual ritual of stoning one member of the community who has won a lottery. This is a fictional depiction of scapegoating that chillingly illustrates the behavior at group level. The act, by those living in the town of stoning the community member, is a literal representation of the act of ridding themselves of unwanted, negative aspects that they wish to deny. The process of scapegoating a group member is both consciously and unconsciously experienced by the group-as-a-whole. A group leader/facilitator that becomes aware of the emergence of scapegoating group behavior should regard it as one aspect of group process. The group leader/facilitator must also act to interpret and interrupt it, in order to heighten the group's awareness and protect the member who is scapegoated.

This chapter has focused on social roles that often develop in groups in the United States. In a global world, it is important to look at social roles beyond the borders of the United States. Following are two examples of social roles—one is in India among the caste of the Dalits, drawn from Viswanath's (2009) work, and the other is among the Jewish population in Israel, taken from the work of Lahav (2009).

In India, the Dalits represent 167 million people, and 220 million in South Asia, who have, for many years, lived an existence in which they have been shunned by members of their society to the rank of untouchables. This means they are at the bottom of India's caste system. The Dalits (which means "broken people") are regarded as permanently impure by birth and they have been and continue to be scapegoated in their society. Discriminated against and oppressed, they represent what has been called India's apartheid. They are continuously relegated to the margins of Indian society, but they are also necessary to the maintenance of that society (Viswanath, 2009, p. 180).

Viswanath (2009) and her colleagues conducted a group relations conference in 2003, titled "Authority, Leadership: Resistance, Self Empowerment and Transformation in Organisational and Social Systems." This conference considered the patterns of internalized oppression among the Dalits that perpetuated unconscious collusion with discriminatory and oppressive societal attitudes and practices. The conference studied Dalit behavior in the context of the broader society by utilizing existing models of Dalit empowerment and applying the group relations model to heighten group-level awareness of patterns of internalized oppression. Based on her conference work with the Dalits, as well as research conducted during post-conference interviews, Viswanath (2009) described the main points of personal learning as follows:

- Recognizing patterns of behavior in oneself and (unconscious) psychological roles
- Focusing on oneself instead of externalizing
- Dealing with and accessing personal authority
- Dealing with the notion of one's own personal authority and that of others
- Recognizing when one is abdicating role—managing self in role and linking role to task
- Recognizing and dealing with anxieties
- Learning how to say no, particularly to those in positions of authority
- Approaching those in authority and engaging with them in assertive manner
- Working with the notion of boundaries as related to task
- Recognizing the notion of a primary task
- Expressing anger
- Releasing blocked energy and transforming the way one is involved in issues
- Realizing that the unconscious was a factor and a layer driving all transactions—being alert and open to this whole new layer
- Being open to diversity (p. 187)

Viswanath (2009) stressed that, although what was learned may seem obvious and somewhat simplistic, it must be contextualized within the systematic and systemic oppression of the Dalits. For example, the ability, at group and individual levels, to express anger in functional ways and to exercise personal authority were "revolutionary and extremely liberating." Viswanath also reported that the act of organizing, conducting, and participating in a conference devoted to the study of caste and discrimination (e.g., more closely associated with unconscious, invisible, and unspeakable dynamics) was an act of defiance and courage among the Dalits.

Another example of the examination of social roles in an international context is the work conducted by Lahav (2009) on Jewish identity. At a group relations conference held in Israel in 2005, Lahav, as the director, along with the staff and members, explored the complexity of social identity and belonging in and between groups of Jewish people in Israel (the name of the state) and the Diaspora (existing in the mind) (Armstrong, 1998, as cited in Lahav, 2009). The systemic challenges explored at the conference relating to Jewish people in Israel concerned questions about whether Judaism is a religion, a nationality, a historical heritage, or a political entity. Also explored was the status of individuals who reside in Israel but are not Jewish. On a broader scale, the Jewish identity regarding Jews in the Diaspora related to the risk of anti-Semitism in Europe, perceived ambivalence regarding support of Israel, as well as processes of assimilation. Leadership and questions of who should control issues of identity and belonging in Israel and the Diaspora were integral parts of the conference's focus.

Those in the conference found that an exploration of social identity dynamics within race or within ethnicity/nationality is often characterized by a higher level of complexity than those that exist between races and/or ethnicities/nationalities. The Jewish members highlighted the need for cultural sensitivity and a dualistic approach to social identity that embodied member experiences of otherness, difference, and adversity, as well as belonging and liberty. Also highlighted was the need to challenge the application of the model dealing with a narrow traditional and stereotypical trait that has historically been attributed to Jewish people (e.g., as victims or as aggressors). The Jewish members also challenged associations with the individualistic, Westernized approaches to the examination of social identity related to power, achievement, and competition as being incompatible with the Jewish identity, which they saw as more collective and with a value of mutual responsibility (Lahav, 2009).

Summary

In this chapter, social roles in groups have been discussed and briefly reviewed. Some of the social roles that are often discussed in regard to groups, such as task-oriented roles, group maintenance roles, and self-centered roles, were described as roles most often identified in groups, such as leader, follower, mediator, rebel, and scapegoat. It is important to consider how social roles impact the lives of individuals in international contexts. We introduced the work of a colleague from India who has been working with the Dalits and the work by a colleague from Israel concerning the Jewish identity. The work of colleagues in India and Israel as well as work conducted by the authors in the United States, emphasizes the importance of recognizing group level identification and an internalization of powerful, pervasive projections that embody the complexities of social roles. Social roles in groups are integrally connected to defense mechanisms of splitting, projection, and projective identification. It is awareness and the capacity to recognize, investigate, explore, and manage these dynamics that promote effective work in groups.

QUESTIONS FOR REVIEW AND DISCUSSION

1. What are the social roles most often taken up by members in groups?

2. What is the impact of projection and projective identification in taking up social roles? Provide some examples from the chapter and/or from your own experiences in groups, or of visual images you have seen (e.g., television shows, movies/films), or books you have read.

3. Define the term *scapegoating* and provide an example of it from a group, a movie you have seen, or a book you have read.

4. How does the work of Viswanath (2009) and Lahav (2009) reflect the importance of social roles at group and societal levels in an international context?

KEY TERMS AND CONCEPTS

Defense mechanisms and role types
Follower
Leader
Mediator
Person-in-role

Rebel/Alternative leader
Role
Scapegoating
Social roles in groups

7

Leadership, Authority, and Power in Racially and Culturally Mixed Groups

This chapter is based on the premise that in many groups and organizations, the race and culture of individuals affect perceptions about their capacity to take up the role of leadership. Racial and cultural identities also affect the ways in which individuals are authorized in the role and the power available to them to fully take up leadership. Those who take up the leader's role as well as those who are members in the group or organization come to the experience with internalized messages about who should and should not be authorized to lead (Alderfer, 1994). These messages are influenced by racial-cultural identity attitudes and cultural values learned in families and communities. These attitudes and values are not usually held in conscious awareness as we interact with others. They are the unspoken messages that linger between "us" and "them." Members and leaders also have the baggage of the histories of conflict and collaboration that have existed between their social identity groups (blacks/whites, Israelis/Palestinians, Serbs/Croatians, etc.). Some members carry and hold on to this baggage, while others do not. Depending on the power of the messages, future generations may be more willing to understand the circumstances of the past and find ways to diminish intergroup tensions. Racial-cultural identity attitudes and cultural values influence how leaders take up their authority. These attitudes and values also affect their authorization in role and the power and influence they hold in providing leadership. The leader and members' racial-cultural identity attitudes and cultural values help shape experiences of leadership, authority, and power in the group and in organizational life.

First, the terms *authority* (e.g., in more detail than provided in Chapter 5), *leadership*, and *power* will be defined. Theories of racial-cultural identity development and cultural values will be briefly introduced. While the focus here is on racial-cultural identity, there are other social identity differences such as religion, social class, age, sexual orientation, and disability that affect perceptions of leadership in groups. Cultural values are discussed as one way of identifying the differences that play a role in leadership, authority, and power in groups. It is the intersection of racial-cultural identity, cultural values, leadership, authority, and power that creates a complexity of emotions and behavior in group and organizational life.

Authority

Authority and leadership are conceptually different (Gastil, 1994; Heifetz & Sinder, 1987). Authority is about position, while leadership is a process of motivating, inspiring, and mobilizing change in groups. Authority refers to a position either formal or informal with the power to make decisions that can be binding on others (Obholzer, 1994). Formal authority is derived from a person's role in a group or organization. For example, the group leader is hired by the clinic to conduct groups on behalf of the clinic that provides space and compensation to the leader for taking up this role. The formal authority to conduct the group is conferred by authority from above, which has the power to continue or terminate the group. The members, who agree to join the group, give approval to the organization and the leader to conduct the group. The members of the group also have the authority not to attend or not to adhere to the rules that they perceive as unjust. This can be considered as "authority from below" (Obholzer, 1994). Those who hold positions of authority usually develop a reputation among those they have worked with that is talked about and passed on as stories about the quality of their performance in given situations (Hoggett, Mayo, & Miller, 2006). Authority by reputation comes from outside the leader and is based on how others perceive or experience them in their role. The leader needs authority from above and below as well as "authority from within" (Obholzer, 1994). Authority from within refers to a sense of personal authority, confidence, and competence that an individual should have to take up the role of leadership.

Heifetz (1994) notes a difference between authority and leadership as those who hold authority do not necessarily exercise leadership. Moreover, individuals without much authority can take up leadership. Heifetz proposes five basic social functions expected of individuals in positions of authority: (1) direction, (2) protection, (3) orientation to role and to place, (4) control of conflict, and (5) maintenance of norms. The expectations of direction for answers to questions, protection from uncomfortable changes that involve gaps between cultural values and the realities of life, and helping individuals remain oriented to current roles are important aspects of leadership and authority. Additionally, rather than confronting new and different roles, maintaining norms, especially ones that are culturally familiar, can offer some level of comfort. However, when one is authorized as a leader, there is some expectation that conflict will be identified as a potential source of creativity. A leader may also be expected to have the capacity to stimulate disorientation on the part of members in order to effect change.

Leadership

Leadership is defined by Parker (2005) as a "negotiated process of mutual influence" (p. 27), suggesting that the leader influences and is influenced by the negotiations that occur in the group. Forsyth (1999) defines leadership as "a special form of social interaction: a reciprocal, transactional, and transformational process in which individuals are permitted to influence and motivate others to promote the attaining of group and individual goals" (p. 343). When members come from different racial-cultural backgrounds, there are often contradictory viewpoints and paradoxical situations that require openness to exploration and working with differences. Members often see the racial-cultural identity of the leader in mixed groups as representing a specific group (e.g., race, ethnicity, gender, sexual orientation, religion, class). If the leader is perceived as being biased, even in subtle and unintentional ways, to a particular subgroup of members, influence is decreased among that subgroup. The leader, very much like President Obama's historic speech on race in 2008, must be able to connect to the multiple identities of the members, valuing each and recognizing the present and historical intergroup concerns. From an organizational perspective, Heifetz (1994) defines leadership as mobilizing others to do adaptive work, which involves working to help understand and work toward the resolution of conflicts in values. He refers to the importance of bridging the gap between cultural values and the context or current conditions in which the group operates. Parker (2005) views leadership as "management of meaning," which involves the mediation and processing of information and effective communication with members and followers. Working effectively with the multiple identities of group members is adaptive work that is required for "meaning making" to emerge, thus mediating cultural divides, reducing conflict, and promoting shared narratives—all functions of leadership that may be particularly key in racial-cultural contexts.

Power

Power may be defined as the "capacity to guide others' actions toward whatever goals are meaningful to the power-holder" (Magee, Gruenfeld, Keltner, & Galinsky, 2004, p. 277). This definition of power suggests that it is a tool or means for the accomplishment of the work of the leader. Thus, the leader has a certain amount of power vested in the role and function. Parker (2005) indicates that the power of the leader is a part of a negotiation process and is shared by those who are the members or followers in the group or organization. Power is also about access to and command of resources as a means to accomplish goals. In groups and organizations, the questions of available resources and who has them are often present and active.

Racial and Cultural Identity Development Theory

RACIAL AND CULTURAL IDENTITY DEVELOPMENT FOR PEOPLE OF COLOR

Racial-cultural identity attitude theorists (Arce, 1981; Atkinson, Morten, & Sue, 1989; Cross, 1994; Helms, 1990, 1995; Kim, 1981; Ponterotto & Pedersen, 1993) developed conceptual models to capture the common experiences of those who experience oppression and those who have the privilege of not dealing with racial-cultural oppression in the United States. Although the models are presented as a stage process, racial-cultural identity for people of color is often conceptualized as a continuous dynamic process. In this process, individuals develop a strong sense of positive identity with their racial-cultural group, moving from identification with the dominant white group to one of pride and acceptance of their own group. While it is important to note the complexity of within- and between-group differences, racial-cultural identity theory provides a conceptual framework for understanding individual attitudes toward one's own and other racial-cultural groups (Sue & Sue, 2008). It provides a lens for understanding how one connects and distances self from one's own and from other racial-cultural groups. Atkinson et al. (1989) capture the stages of most of the racial identity theories in their five stages of minority identity development, from a strong identification with the dominant white middle class to an appreciation of one's own racial-cultural group. They define three attitudes: (1) attitudes toward others in the same reference group, (2) attitudes toward others in different minority groups, and (3) attitudes toward the dominant or majority white group. Table 7.1 provides an overview of the racial-cultural identity development model.

TABLE 7.1 Racial-Cultural Identity Development Model

Stage of Minority Development	Attitude Toward Others of Same Minority	Attitude Toward Others of a Different Minority	Attitude Toward Dominant Group
Conformity	Self-depreciating, low salience of race	Discriminatory behavior	Group appreciating
Dissonance and appreciating	Conflict between attitudes of group appreciation and depreciation (questioning, inquiry, reality checking)	Conflict between views held by dominant group and feelings of shared experience (questioning, inquiry, reality checking)	Conflict between group attitudes of appreciating and depreciating of dominant group (questioning, inquiry, reality checking)
Resistance and immersion	Attitudes of group appreciation of own racial-cultural group	Conflict between sense of empathy with other minority groups and feelings of ethnocentrism	Attitudes of group depreciation, dominant group seen as oppressor
Introspection	Sorting out individual beliefs from those of the group, searching for balance between belonging to subgroup and world citizenship	Concern about ethnocentric judgments, interest in learning about the oppression and experiences of others	Concern about group depreciation, decrease in feelings of distrust, anger, and generalizations of the entire group
Integrative awareness	Group appreciation, sense of pride in group, ability to question and disagree with certain beliefs and values without fear of alienation	Group appreciation, attempt to understand cultural values and ways of life Supportive of other oppressed groups	Selective appreciation and trust of certain members of dominant groups who seek to eliminate oppression

SOURCE: Adapted from Derald Wing Sue and David Sue (2008). *Counseling the Culturally Diverse: Theory and Practice*, 5th ed. Hoboken, NJ: John Wiley & Sons.

WHITE RACIAL AND CULTURAL IDENTITY ATTITUDES

Helms's (1995) model of white racial identity attitudes is most widely cited in the literature. The assumption of this model is that racism is an integral part of the white American experience. To develop a healthy white identity, one must abandon racism and develop a nonracist white identity. Helms identified six racial identity statuses: (1) contact, (2) disintegration, (3) reintegration, (4) pseudoindependence, (5) immersion/emersion, and (6) autonomy. Similar to the minority identity theorists, she refers to these statuses as more descriptive of the dynamic processes related to attitudes, behavior, and human emotions. Status indicates that a person does not move from one stage to the other in sequence but evolves in more cyclical ways, depending on the context and situation. The following is a brief review of the white identity ego statuses and information-processing strategies drawn from Helms's work:

1. *Contact:* People in this status are satisfied with the status quo and are oblivious to racism. They believe in meritocracy, believe that everyone is equal, and have little or no experience with inequality.

2. *Disintegration:* Experience anxiety with unresolved racial and moral dilemmas, feel that they must choose between loyalty to own group and nonwhite groups. It results in ambivalence and suppression of emotions.

3. *Reintegration:* There is an idealization of white racial group and a denigration and intolerance of other groups. Fear, anger, and hostility are exhibited toward other groups. There is negative distortion of other groups.

4. *Pseudoindependence:* Sincere curiosity about other groups, intellectualized commitment to one's own racial group, and misleading sense of tolerance for other groups. There is reconsideration of perceptions of other groups and reality.

5. *Immersion/emersion:* Search to understand racism and the ways in which it positively and negatively affects the lives of the members of one's own group and the lives of others. There is a pull to redefine what it means to be white. It is more alert and attentive to racism.

6. *Autonomy:* Emotional and intellectual appreciation for racial ethnic differences, positive commitment to one's own racial group, capacity to let go of racial privileges, and to avoid participating in racial oppression. It is more understanding of complexity and more flexible.

The leader and each member enter the group with racial-cultural identity attitudes about preferences toward their own racial-cultural group and other groups. These attitudes can be enacted consciously and unconsciously in behavioral interactions, comments, nonverbal behaviors, and slights of varying levels. Topics concerning racial and cultural issues evoke reactions that can be intense, and feelings of guilt and shame can be easily activated. The fear of exposure to being perceived as racist, ethnocentric, sexist, homophobic, or classist in a "multicultural society" is considered socially and politically incorrect and potentially dangerous for career aspirations of both the leader and the members. A general example of this was the 2008 presidential primary elections in the United States, in which the press, with some assistance from the rival political party's spokesperson, attempted to label Barack Obama as holding racist attitudes because of his association with the minister of his church, Reverend Jeremiah Wright. The assumption was that all African Americans hold similar racial-cultural identity attitudes. Thus, Obama could not belong to a church and be at a different status of racial-cultural identity from that of his pastor. The racial-cultural backgrounds and generational differences between Reverend Wright and President Obama strongly influenced their racial-cultural identity attitudes.

Given the history of the black church in the struggle for civil rights and social justice for people of African descent, Obama was in the precarious position of having to choose between his racial and spiritual family group and that of the broader U.S. constituency. He chose the Janus-like role of looking both internally and externally (e.g., looking inward and outward simultaneously), thus "becoming both participant and observer" (Turquet, 1985, p. 73). As an observer, he was able to glide above the fray and provide observations of behaviors, thoughts, and feelings of the various subgroups. His speech on race noted the negative stereotypes and biases that exist among each group while making note of the points of joining and working on behalf of the whole. As a participant, he provided narratives from personal experiences (e.g., his biracial identity and his relationship with his white maternal grandmother, who loved him yet held racist beliefs about black males), all of which allowed him to reflect on the complexity of having been on both sides of the racial divide.

President Obama's speech acknowledged the racial problems people face in the United States (the group-as-a-whole), and his candid sharing of prejudices from both white and black members of society demonstrated his connection to and disappointment with racial attitudes on both sides. He was also able to hold on to the pride of his African and African American identity and to his pride of being nurtured and cared for by his white mother, grandparents, relatives, and the broader community. President Obama demonstrated that he was in the integrative awareness stage of racial identity. In this stage, the individual has an appreciation for others of the same and different racial minority groups and for those from the dominant group. His ability to communicate this appreciation provided hope to a large number of citizens from different racial-cultural identity groups and fostered their capacity to authorize him in his role as a presidential candidate. The sociologist Ruth Hill has coined the term *Third Culture* for children who have grown up in more than one culture. President Obama would be considered a Third-Culture person since he lived with his family in Indonesia. Perhaps, it is his broader cultural view that shaped his ability to connect across cultures. As more people travel, live, and experience different cultures, increased awareness and understanding may occur among, between, and within cultural groups.

CULTURAL VALUES

Racial-cultural identity development may be more central to those born in the United States and other countries with a strong emphasis on race. However, cultural values and the identification of "the other," which represents the pull for dominance of one group over the other, seem to be universal. Kluckhohn and Strodtbeck (1961) developed a model for understanding how cultural values differed among cultural groups. They provide five different areas of relationship dimensions:

1. *People to nature/environment:* mastery or harmony

2. *Time orientation:* past, present, and future

3. *People relations:* lineal, individual, or collective

4. *Mode of activity:* doing, being, and becoming

5. *Human nature:* good or bad

Sue and Sue (2008) compared the cultural values of different racial-cultural groups. In some cultures, people are more focused on the past; in some, on the present; and in others, on the future. Cultures also differ in attitudes about human activity, in terms of doing, being, and being-in-becoming. They also differ in valuing social relations as lineal, individualistic, or collateral; and in the views of human nature as being either good or bad. Some cultures see people as living in harmony with nature, while others think it most important to have mastery over nature. For example, Asians are considered more collectively oriented in their cultural values than Americans of European descent who are more individualist. These five dimensions of cultural values help frame how people see and experience leadership, authority, and power in groups and organizations. Leaders and members who are focused on the past may use past experiences as a reference for making decisions and may have difficulty responding to a call for leadership that involves detailed planning and change for the future. Leaders and members who are more individualistic in their values may consider individual needs before those of the collective group. The economic crisis of 2008 has been attributed to the individualistic orientation of some U.S. business executives who put their personal greed before the needs of their companies and communities.

LEADERSHIP IN RACIALLY AND CULTURALLY MIXED GROUPS

Leadership in racially and culturally mixed groups involves a form of orchestration of conflicting and competing cultural values and racial identity attitudes of group members, allowing space for acknowledging, engaging, and valuing multiple perspectives (Heifetz, 1994). According to Heifetz, leaders are expected to maintain some equilibrium of roles and norms for the groups they lead. They are expected to work successfully with the identity politics of difference in a way that is productive and, it is hoped, transformative. Group members expect the leader to help lower their anxiety and apprehension about being in a group (Kline, 2003). There is an expectation that the leader understands what will happen in the group and provide some guidance to the members. Both the leader and the members enter the group with racial identity attitudes and cultural values that provide a lens for their perception of the leadership role. When the leader is from a disenfranchised group, there are some stereotypes that may affect member expectations and projections of how this person takes up the role. If the leader is not at a mature racial identity status and is not confident in her or his role as leader, she or he may act in a manner that feels incongruent with the role of leadership (McRae, 2004). If the leader and group members hold different cultural values and have no awareness of how to work with these differences, potential conflict and misunderstanding may occur.

Leadership, authority, and authorization are related to the expectations of who should take up leadership and the characteristics associated with the role of a leader. These expectations, along with unconscious processes related to anxiety or apprehension about the racial-cultural identity of the person in the leader's role, exist in most groups. For instance, a group with predominantly Muslim members may have difficulty authorizing a Jewish leader. The long history of racial, cultural, and religious differences may make it difficult to trust that the leader will protect Muslim group members. Cultural values, stereotypes, and racial-cultural attitudes often shape our expectations of who is capable of taking up leadership roles in a group and organization.

The leader and each member enter the group with their own racial identity attitudes that influence their lens for engaging with others. In mixed groups, Tsui (1997) reports that Asian members at the conformity stage may side with white members and say denigrating things about their own cultural group. He suggests that this overidentification with white clients provides an opportunity for the leader to help them explore projections and discuss their struggle to adapt to the dominant culture. If the leader is at a similar racial identity status as the clients, they may be pulled to identify with that subgroup, which can polarize the group. Groups are most productive when the leader has a more mature racial identity status than the members (Helms, 1990).

Awareness and acceptance of differences and some understanding of the cultural values of other groups that are being worked with provide a good basic foundation for taking up a leader's role in racially and culturally mixed groups. In Table 7.2, some of the expectations and projections that members have for leaders are outlined. Tasks of the leader, based on the racial-cultural context of the group, are also outlined. Table 7.2 provides a conceptual framework for

TABLE 7.2 Leadership Tasks and Members' Expectations

Group Context	Expectations and Projections of the Leader	Leader's Tasks
White leader Mostly white and a few members of color	White members: *Contact, disintegration, and reintegration*—may expect the leader to collude with them in stereotypes and projections of people of color; little desire to discuss differences. *Pseudoindependence, immersion, and autonomy*—expect the leader and other members to work with difference. People of color: *Conformity*—will identify with the leader and white members and attempt to make differences invisible. *Resistance/immersion*—will not expect the leader to protect them from dominant member's potential attacks. Projections of power and authority associated with the leader and the white members *Introspection/integrative awareness*—will expect the leader and members to be fair when working with differences until experience otherwise. Cultural values: Majority members may expect more focus on individual preferences than that of the group. Those in minority may work with the collective in mind and expect the leader to consider collective before individual; majority may focus attention to taking action and working for a better future.	Inquire about verbal and nonverbal behavior, acknowledge the power differences, and be curious with the group about how they are manifested in the group's behavior. Be careful not to allow difference to be *only* in people of color. Work with projections onto the leader and members as they are applicable to the group's dynamics. Be aware of the different cultural values of members and how they influence interpersonal and group dynamics.
White leader Mostly people of color and a few white members	People of color: *Resistance/immersion*—may expect that their numbers are insignificant to the authority of a white leader; they may feel that they won't be seen or heard; may conceal or highlight their differences to test safety with the leader (fight/flight).	Inquire about verbal and nonverbal behaviors; acknowledge the complexity of power differences. Help members to explore the

Group Context	Expectations and Projections of the Leader	Leader's Tasks
	White members: *Disintegration and reintegration*—may see the presence of the white leader as key for maintaining leadership and power. Projections of the leader as caring and identifying more for one group than the other. Cultural values: Members of color may expect the leader to address their concerns as a collective more readily, or they may see the leader as a representative of her or his racial group with little interest in the cultural views of the members and more comfortable with being-in-becoming than doing or taking actions quickly; focus on past events may be a way of working with the present.	meaning of their experience and find out how it is related to life outside the group. Work with projections of the leader as they are applicable to the group's dynamics. Be aware of the different cultural values of members.
Latino leader Mostly white and a few Latino members	White members: *Contact, disintegration, reintegration, pseudoindependence, and immersion*—may expect lack of credentials and project incompetence onto the leader. *Autonomy*—may expect the leader and other members to work with difference. Latinos: *Conformity*—will identify with the leader and white members and attempt to make differences invisible. *Resistance/immersion*—will not expect the leader to protect them from potential attacks. Latino members, depending on racial/ethnic identity, may join white members or expect the leader to be more protective of them. Advanced status identity members may join or overidentify with the leader.	Inquire about member feeling and thoughts about authority and what it means to have a Latino in this role, acknowledging different perspectives. Protect Latina/Latino members from being scapegoated as a deflection from projections onto the leader. Speak about expectations and projections in a nonjudgmental way. Work with projections onto the leader as they are applicable to the group's dynamics.

(Continued)

103

TABLE 7.2 (Continued)

Group Context	Expectations and Projections of the Leader	Leader's Tasks
	Cultural values: Majority members may expect the leader to abide by the cultural values of the dominant class. May see the leader as having joined their group by taking up such a role. Minority members may also expect the leader to follow the majority rules. The leader may be perceived as having strayed away from ethnic culture to fit into the dominant group.	Be aware of the different cultural values of members and the perceptions that members might have about the cultural values of the leader.
Latino leader Mostly Latino and a few white members	**Latinos:** *Dissonance and resistance*—may expect the leader to identify and collude with them in taking up voice and leadership in the group. Among Latino members' language fluency, bi- and multilingualism may be linked with competence and authority. Within-group ethnic differences may emerge among Latino members as they relate to power, privilege, acculturation, and assimilation. **White members:** *Disintegration, reintegration, and psuedoindependence*—may be cautious about being heard and understood. **Cultural values:** Latino members may expect the leader to be more collective than individually oriented and more comfortable with being-in-becoming than doing or taking actions quickly; focus on past events may be a way of working with the present.	Inquire about member feelings and thoughts about authority and what it means to have a Latino in this role, acknowledging the number of Latino members and inquiring what this reversal of minority/majority means for the group. Speak about expectations and projections in a nonjudgmental way. Protect white members from attack. Work with the projections onto the leader, as they are applicable to the group's dynamics. Be careful of overidentification with members. Be aware of the different cultural values of members

Group Context	Expectations and Projections of the Leader	Leader's Tasks
Asian leader Mostly white and a few Asian members	White members: *Contact, disintegration, reintegration, pseudoindependence*—expect the leader to be passive and lacking in leadership skills in accordance with stereotypes ascribed to Asians in leadership roles; projections of passivity onto leader. Asian members: *Resistance and immersion*—expect clear boundaries of authority to be set by the leader, and expect the leader to identify with their cause and be more supportive of their subgroup; may withdraw into silence if uncomfortable (Tsui, 1997). Cultural values: Majority members may expect the leader to conform to their cultural values. Minority members may be disappointed if the leader does not demonstrate an understanding and connection to subgroup cultural values.	Display confidence and empathic understanding. Inquire about power dynamics and expectations of the leader's role. Acknowledge differences and seek to make meaning of different perspectives. Protect Asian members from being scapegoated as a deflection from projections onto the leader. Work with the projections of the leader as they are applicable to the group's dynamics. Be aware of the different cultural values of members.
Asian leader Mostly Asian and a few white members	Asian members: *Resistance and immersion*—may feel more empowered by the numbers and expect the leader to collude with them in terms of power dynamics. *Introspection and integrative awareness*—expect the leader to take up authority role and exercise leadership for all members of the group; projections of competence onto the leader. White members: *Immersion/emersion and autonomy*—may expect the leader to take up role in fair and just manner. Lower statuses may project feelings of inadequacy in taking up leadership role.	Inquire about complex power dynamics and expectations of the leader's role. Display availability to all members. Create atmosphere to help all members feel safe enough to discuss their concerns. Work with the projections on the leader as they are applicable to the group's dynamics.

(Continued)

TABLE 7.2 (Continued)

Group Context	Expectations and Projections of the Leader	Leader's Tasks
	Language fluency, bi- and multilingualism may be linked with competence and authority among Asian members. Within-group ethnic differences may emerge among Asian members related to power, privilege, acculturation, and assimilation. Cultural values: Many members may be more collective than individually oriented toward the group work and more comfortable with being-in-becoming than doing or taking actions quickly; focus on past events may be a way of working with the present.	Be careful of overidentification with members from the same subgroup. Be aware of the different cultural values and the impact of language on members.
Black leader Mostly white and a few black members	White members: *Disintegration, reintegration, and pseudoindependence*—expect that black people will be given preference. Black members: *Resistance and immersion*—may strongly identify with the leader and expect a level of protection as a minority in a group. Stereotypes of competence and validity; projections of anger, hostility, protector, and caretaker toward black women leaders; projections of aggression on black men leaders; surprise and/or suspicion regarding the leader's competence. Cultural values: Majority members expect the leader to conform to dominant cultural rules and values. Minority members expect to see some demonstration of valuing the culture of their subgroup.	Inquire about verbal and nonverbal behaviors, acknowledging the roles, power differences, and being curious with the group about how differences are manifested in group's behavior. Explore feelings and thoughts about the impact of roles on behavior. Help to attribute meaning to experience. Protect black members from being scapegoated as a deflection from projections onto the leader.

Group Context	Expectations and Projections of the Leader	Leader's Tasks
		Work with the projections of the leader as they are applicable to the group's dynamics. Be aware of the different cultural values of members.
Black leader

Mostly black and a few white members | Black members:

Resistance, immersion, introspection, and integrative awareness—expect to be heard and opinions respected by the leader.

White members:

Immersion/emersion—cautious about being heard and opinions respected.

White members may feel anxious regarding the perceived shift in the balance of power and privilege. Black members may begin to differentiate based on ethnic, social class, and other cultural differences.

Stereotypes of competence and validity; projections of anger, hostility, protector, and caretaker toward black women leaders; projections of aggression on black men leaders; surprise and/or suspicion regarding the leader's competence; competition with the leader.

Cultural values:

Majority of members may be more collective than individually oriented and expect the leader to display similar values. | Inquire about verbal and nonverbal behaviors acknowledging the roles, power differences, and being curious with the group about how they are manifested in the group's behavior. Explore feelings and thoughts about the impact of roles on behavior. Help attribute meaning to experience.

Protect white members from attack. Work with the projections of the leader as they are applicable to the group's dynamics. Be careful of overidentification with members.

Be aware of different cultural values of members. |

SOURCE: Helms (1995); Kluckhohn and Strodtbeck (1961); Sue and Sue (2008).

understanding members' expectations when the leader is from a similar or different racial-cultural background and when the ratio of group members varies. This table was developed from conversations with colleagues, the literature, and personal and professional experiences of the authors. An assumption is that when the leader is from a Latino and/or a black racial-cultural minority group, the expectations and projections are more reflective of incompetence. For blacks, because of the role of slavery, this idea is drawn from the works of Toni Morrison, who cites black, Latino, and other people of color as having a history of being of service to others (E. Holvina, personal communication, August 8, 2008). For Asian leaders, the expectations and projections are around passivity and lack of leadership skills. Expectations and projections will vary for the racial identity attitudes of the members from the same or different racial-cultural groups.

Case Examples

In a group that consisted of a white male consultant/leader and a predominantly white membership, there was a reluctance to discuss racial-cultural differences. The group found it easier to discuss racial and cultural issues outside the group, as if they were unrelated to their here-and-now experiences. Members told stories about their earlier experiences. The consultant/leader asked, "How do we bring it [the discussion] into the here and now rather than talk about school day stories?" This intervention helped one of the two African Americans speak about his experience:

> Being an African American, I'm generally accustomed to being attacked and having my thoughts [considered] just being out of line. So essentially being here, my heart's like racing because I'm ready to like fend off whatever is going to come at me next. I'm ready to do battle. You know I was talking about it with one of my friends this morning. It kind of sucks to always be this tough warrior and it's exhausting. I wish I could show people that I can be weak. I wish I could show people that I have a heart. I'm afraid I'll be destroyed. Because being a black male, I feel as though I've spent my entire life experience carrying negative projections. So to a certain extent, I have to be rugged in order not to collapse. But that's not all of who I am.

As the conversation continued, the other black man who was older talked about being more acutely aware of his aging. Another man, who was white, spoke of being gay:

> As a gay man who was a gay child, who was alone in his world, it is a completely different experience because you can hide it. But man, it's a rough one because you can hide it and you damn fucking well better.

The consultant/leader's intervention authorized the members to bring the conversation into the room and speak about their own experiences and concerns about how the group might relate to them. At this point, the members felt safe enough to converse about the fears of race, aging, and homosexuality. The consultant/leader's intervention let the members know that he was ready to hear their stories, and perhaps, they were also ready to hear each other's stories. The consultant/leader in this group was an older white male who had demonstrated his appreciation for all the members, despite a pull to join only with the white members of the group. This exchange also demonstrates how members make alliances within and across race and culture. In this case, the connection was based on experiences of oppression across race, age, and sexual orientation.

In an experiential fishbowl group of eight students in a class, a Jewish woman and a Muslim woman began to talk about the cultural differences between them. Another member quickly intervened, stating that there were other differences in the group as well. Two other members joined her in taking the group's focus away from the two members who represented a powerful difference in the group. The consultant/leader intervened,

> I wonder if the Jewish/Muslim differences are too hot for exploration in this group. What are some of the fears of what might happen if the conversation between these two members continued?

The consultant/leader is encouraging the members to examine their fears around the ethnic and religious boundaries held by the members of the group and what it would mean for these two members to discuss their cultural differences.

In a small study group where more than half of the 12 members were Latino, the Latino members spent the first 20 minutes monopolizing the group by talking about their experiences as immigrants and of being forced to change their names by priests and guidance counselors who were seemingly unable to pronounce them. They focused on how their cultural values had changed over time and how they were now able to exert more power over certain aspects of their identities, including their names. In this case, their identification with the Latino consultant/leader enhanced their ability to take control of the group. The other members who were mostly white members sat quietly observing. The Latino consultant/leader asked,

> What is the message that the Latinos are sending to other members in this group and why is there no space for other voices? Perhaps the Latinos in this group now have the power to change the course of things?

In this example, the consultant/leader is inquiring about the behavior of the group and trying to help them make sense of their behavior by focusing on their behavior and its purpose. He draws attention to the cultural subgroups and the power differential among them, a situation that is not common for most of the members, since Latinos are a minority. He also invites the other members from different subgroups to engage in the exploration and conversation.

The issue of power will surface in mixed groups in different ways. The awareness of race, privilege, and the power to set standards is exemplified in a comment from a young black man in a group:

> I think, the comment was made again, which I think is so relevant here, that, as someone with power privilege, that just comes with being a white man in this society, and how this society was formed, that it's easy for you not to see the power. That's a privilege that you have. Because it's such a given. It happens every day. For me, let me illustrate my point with a story: I worked in a Christmas store one year. And I'd never thought about it, until a woman came in one day and asked for a dark-haired angel. I never, ever thought about it, and I looked around the store, and we happened to have one, and she nearly fell on her knees, thanking me, and it wasn't until then I thought about the fact being the majority of the angels you see displayed in this country are blond-haired angels, and so, it was, it helped me move the question of race a little further up, What is it like to be a white girl, a little white girl, with dark hair, and see that all angels have blond hair? What does that say about me? And so, it's just from the fact that you're able to move about in this culture on a daily basis and see yourself reflected. See your experience reflected. And it is held up as the standard; that invests a certain level of power and privilege. Therefore, those of us who don't meet that standard have to be inventive, to find our way into those pictures.

Sampson (1993) purported that the dominant cultural group has the power to set the standard for discourse and behavior. This member addressed his realization of this power in this narrative.

Another comment made by a woman in a small study group is indicative of the kinds of feelings and concerns that exist in some mixed racial-cultural groups around power differences:

> I think just identifying the power dynamic, how things work and how things are and identifying it, and sometimes, yes, things are fucked up. Honestly, people do hate other people, and as bad as we don't want to look at it, sometimes that's just the reality. Some people see it more than others, and some people just have to deal with it.

This woman voiced what often feels unspeakable in groups (White, 2002). The fear that one will be hated for having more or less resources and power is ever present. Groups that are racially and culturally mixed can potentially become polarized between those who are dominant or the majority either in the group or in society and those who have access to more resources or power. Each person enters a group with her or his own attitudes and beliefs about who should and should not have power; often these beliefs are covert and enacted unintentionally. Miller (1985) warned that every transaction across boundaries of political identity has the potential for disaster. He purported that there is a fantasized boundary between how a person sees "me" and "not me" that may not stand the test of reality. Inquiry and meaning making involves working across the boundary of "me" and "not me," identifying points of collaboration and competition, and working to understand the processes that promote and prevent connections (Jordan, 2001).

During the initial sessions of mixed groups, when members are getting to know each other, they may create familiar alliances related to race and culture. However, as their comfort with each other increases, alliances outside their racial-cultural group emerge more prominently (McRae, 1994). The authors have found that in mixed racial-cultural groups, members of African and Latino descent often feel empowered when the leader is of the same racial-cultural background. This can be true for groups that are predominantly lesbian, gay, bisexual, transgender, as well as queer groups. The leader, whether she or he chooses to or not, becomes a representative of a social identity group. The question is similar to the one faced by Obama when he was a presidential candidate, "Is leadership taken up for one subgroup or the group-as-a-whole?" Another question is "How does one communicate with a group in a way that does not polarize the members and isolate the communicator?" The leader needs to be prepared to confront and challenge the group to work with differences and similarities and apply her or his learning to situations outside the group. Ivey, Pedersen, and Ivey (2001) note that inquiry about cultural, environmental, and contextual issues will increase a group's awareness of how the then and there or outside life experiences affect the here and now of the group's immediate experience.

Acknowledging and accepting differences will help the group members become more aware of their cultural attitudes, be more understanding of the worldviews of others, and develop culturally appropriate skills (Mio, Barker-Hackett, & Tumambing, 2009).

The designated leader or consultant of the group holds power with her or his position of authority in the group. Members from different racial-cultural groups will respond to the power of this role according to their cultural values and their racial identity attitudes.

Summary

This chapter defined and discussed leadership, authority, and power in groups. Theories of racial-cultural identity attitudes and cultural values as a framework for understanding their influence on how the leader and members are authorized in role in groups and organizations are presented. This conceptual framework can be helpful in examining the relatedness of the individuals' racial-cultural identities to their own and to other groups. Racial-cultural identity attitudes and cultural values shape the expectations of the leaders and members about the authority and leadership potential in the group. Table 7.2 provides a conceptual framework to help readers learn about group context, expectations of the leader, and the leader's tasks.

QUESTIONS FOR REVIEW AND DISCUSSION

1. What is the definition of leadership, authority, and power that works best for you?

2. Discuss how you understand the terms *leader* and *leadership*? Consider the issue of person and process.

3. How do racial-cultural identity attitudes affect the leader's role? Consider your answer from the perspective of those who have been disenfranchised and those who have not.

4. How do cultural values affect leader and member interactions?

5. Think of a group you have observed and use the concepts from this chapter to describe and analyze the group experience.

KEY TERMS AND CONCEPTS

Acknowledgment and acceptance of differences

Authority

Cultural values

Leadership

Leadership in racially and culturally mixed groups

People of color racial-cultural identity development

Power

Racial-cultural identity development

White racial-cultural identity attitudes

8

Strategies for Leadership in Multicultural Groups

This chapter focuses on the strategies and competencies required to maintain the leader role and implement the tasks of the group. Some of the questions to be explored are as follows: (a) What are the competencies required for effective leadership? (b) What are some effective group-level interventions? (c) What are the appropriate strategies for intervening with groups when the members come from different racial and cultural backgrounds? The leaders' awareness and understanding of within-group differences, such as racial/ethnic identity attitudes, along with cultural values, social class, and biases, will influence strategies of working with groups. As has been stated throughout this book, groups that consist of members from different racial and cultural backgrounds are complex entities. The complexity of multiple identities and experiences of individuals in groups requires a level of competence from the group leader, if she or he is to lead or facilitate the group effectively.

In this chapter, we introduce a set of competencies developed by the A. K. Rice Institute for the Study of Social Systems (AKRI). These competencies were developed for the Consultant Training and Certification Program of AKRI by a team of experts. The competencies are presented here, with the organization's permission, because they encompass the basic leadership skills while providing an in-depth view of the range of skills necessary when working with groups with members from different racial and cultural backgrounds.

The AKRI Competencies

The AKRI competencies were originally developed for individuals working as consultants at group relations conferences; they are adapted in this chapter for group leaders who work with a variety of groups. In adapting these competencies, we incorporate the cultural competencies described by Ivey, Pedersen, and Ivey (2001) and by Sue and Sue (2008) for professionals: (a) awareness of the group leader's own assumptions, values, and biases; (b) understanding the worldview of other racial-cultural groups; and (c) developing appropriate intervention strategies and techniques. This chapter focuses on the third competency, the development of strategies and skills in working effectively with groups that consist of members from different racial-cultural backgrounds. In light of the state of the world's economy, the work of Heifetz (1994) on leadership as an adaptive force that mobilizes communities to tackle difficult problems will also be addressed. Leadership in mixed-race groups requires a form of what Heifetz refers to as "orchestration of competing perspectives." Finally, the chapter provides examples of how these competencies can be applied in groups.

Hayden and Carr (1993), who initiated the development of training competencies for consultants in AKRI group relations conferences, addressed the need for a consultant's "dedication to scrutinizing his or her own accuracy" (p. 93). This involves acknowledging when errors are made and recognizing that this is an important part of the task of leadership of a group. It models for members that they are not expected to be perfect, that mistakes can be made, and that there is an opportunity for recovery in the group. Hayden and Carr warn us that leaders who persist in the pursuit of their personal goals, whether they are emotional or intellectual, are in violation of the task and role of leadership. Thus, leaders need to take care of their personal needs in their own therapy, not in the groups they are working with.

AKRI has developed a set of prerequisite competencies for those who are interested in taking up the consultant role. These competencies can be helpful as assessment criteria for professors or training directors who are helping prepare group workers. In what follows, we list the competencies as they were written by AKRI associates and then provide a brief explanation for adapting them to group work in various settings. The prerequisite competencies are listed with brief comments about how they can be identified and developed in a basic group dynamics course. The competencies are divided into two stages, Stage 1 and Stage 2. Stage 1 is a requirement for those who are consultants-in-training, and Stage 2 is for certification as a conference consultant. The AKRI competencies entail the leader's capacity to both self-examine and work with the group's dynamics. These are two processes that occur simultaneously, each helping the other work more effectively with the group.

Many counselor education and psychology programs provide only one course in group dynamics, with limited focus on the development of skills and competencies required for working with groups. A basic course can assess and help students develop prerequisite and Stage 1 competencies, and a more advanced course can be used for actual practice and application of skills.

Practice, application of techniques, and supervision facilitate the development of competence in group work. In what follows, the prerequisites are adapted to show Stage 1 and Stage 2 competencies, as has been done in the group dynamics classes that we have taught over the years. The competencies will be explained in more detail, and examples of leader interventions that demonstrate how the competencies can be applied in group work will be provided.

PREREQUISITE COMPETENCIES

The six competencies that are considered as prerequisite for those who plan to lead groups are similar to the attending and basic listening skills described by Ivey et al. (2001). These are the foundation on which the AKRI Stage 1 and Stage 2 competencies are built:

- The ability to be reflective and self-examining
- An understanding that the task of the consultant/leader is to further the learning of the group, with a focus on authority relations
- The embodiment of genuine curiosity about what is happening in the group as a whole
- An acceptance that the experience of others is as valid as one's own
- The capacity to work collaboratively with the experiences of others in understanding the group as a whole
- The capacity to be vulnerable in service of one's own learning and the learning of the group

The first competency, the ability to be reflective and self-examining, involves group leaders being reflective of what is going on in the group and attentive to their own feelings, which might influence their interventions and members' behavior in the group. Heifetz and Linsky (2002) refer to the leader as being in the group and on the balcony at the same time. They state that staying with the group allows the leader to attend to the feelings, tensions, and joys of the here-and-now experience of the group. Being on the balcony creates some distance to observe interactions with a more objective eye and distinguish one's own feelings from those of group members. The second competency concerns furthering the group's learning with a focus on authority relations. Many of the interactions between group members from different racial-cultural backgrounds are related to authority and power relations, such as issues of dependency, fight/flight, or counterdependency. The group members learn from exploring authority relations with each other and from application to experiences outside the group. Being genuinely curious about the group's process, as specified in the third competency, consists of the leader recognizing that the group is an entity, with a life that is composed of developmental and dynamic phases. A group leader's focus needs to be primarily on the group-as-a-whole, as opposed to individual group members. In keeping with this perspective, a group leader's expression of curiosity about the group-as-a-whole allows members to focus on roles and projective processes at the individual, group, and systemic level. This is the power of group work.

The fourth competency encompasses multicultural skills and involves the ability of the leader to be aware of the worldviews of the members in the group. It also requires the leader's ability to facilitate and make interventions about the group's process in appropriate ways. Acknowledging the validity of others' experience requires the capacity to explore the lenses through which others see the world. A willingness to work collaboratively with the experiences of others, which is the fifth competency, often follows this type of acknowledgment. Collaboration between members can also be affected by competition within groups. Competition among group members is often expressed in the form of conflict; racial-cultural differences can contribute to the intensity of competitive, conflicted interactions within the group. However, competition is not necessarily dichotomous from collaboration; on the contrary, it can often be a covert form of group member collaboration. Thus, competition within groups is not inherently negative. Competition is a necessary aspect of group life; it can help group members enhance levels of awareness and provide more in-depth interactions and skills. It can also help the group evolve, developmentally. The fifth competency, the capacity to be vulnerable in service of self- and group learning, is based on our belief that acquiring and working with these prerequisite competencies requires a certain amount of vulnerability on the part of the leader. In our work with groups, we have noticed that people who are more reflective and self-aware are often more willing to be vulnerable. The ability to be vulnerable as a group leader is a form of risk taking that models for members who may feel anxious and fearful about their own vulnerability. It also communicates that the group is a safe enough place to engage in risk-taking behavior. Heifetz (1994) refers to developing relationships that provide a holding environment where members feel a level of trust in the leader.

STAGE 1 AND STAGE 2 COMPETENCIES

The AKRI competencies are those required for a group worker who has demonstrated competence in the prerequisites. Individuals develop competence differently; thus, proficiency in competencies will vary. We list some of the competencies below and provide examples of a number of them that illustrate both the development and the use of the competencies:

- The capacity to maintain task and role boundaries in the face of positive or negative responses from others
- An understanding that taking up authority may include tolerating loneliness, derision, or being misunderstood

- The ability to reflect on and express one's internal experience rather than acting on it
- A respectful and curious stance toward others' learning and experience
- The courage to speak what is felt to be unspeakable in the particular work context as long as it relates to the task of the group at hand
- The ability to recognize that individuals "carry" or express some aspect of the experience of the group as a whole, for example, scapegoating and rescuing
- An appreciation of the range and complexity of unconscious activity
- The capacity to adapt role behavior to suit the task of the group
- An understanding that the exercise of leadership and representation affects, and is affected by, group and intergroup dynamics
- An understanding of how organizational dynamics reflect the larger socio-political context
- The ability to shift one's attention to consider intrapsychic, interpersonal, group, and intergroup perspectives in order to understand what is happening in the group as a whole
- An understanding of how elements of one's own identity and history affect one's work, as well as calling forth of particular fantasies and projections from others in the context of groups
- An understanding of how one's own experience in role relates to the working environment as a whole
- The ability to formulate group-level unconscious processes as they are occurring using words, images, analogies, and metaphors
- The capacity for self-containment and the ability to "hold still" emotionally long enough to identify and feel along the boundary between what resides in the group and the environment and what resides in one's self
- The ability to regain the consultant role after it has been lost
- The ability to facilitate members' application of group learning to their experiences in other contexts

Competencies

- *The capacity to maintain task and role boundaries in the face of positive or negative responses from others*

- *The capacity to adapt role behavior to suit the task of the group*

- *An understanding of how one's own experience in role relates to the working environment as a whole*

It is the responsibility of the group leader to keep the task of the group in mind, to share observations, and to explore group behavior that takes the group off task. In addition to maintaining the task, the group leader manages role boundaries such as time, territory, and the diverse personalities of the group members. The complexity of these factors can challenge the leader's ability to maintain his or her role in the group. Leaders have different perceptions of their authority and leadership role, which will affect the ways in which they respond to the group's challenge of their authority. For example, leaders who have a strong desire to be liked by members may have difficulty maintaining their role when the group members make negative comments or demonstrate their dislike for something the leader has said. The pull to please the members may blur the boundaries between leader and member roles, making it difficult for the leader to recognize the underlying dynamic of dependency and fight/flight in the group. Leaders who are aware of their valence to be liked are more able to reflect and separate personal needs from those of the group. In the example that follows, the consultant/leader is being challenged by the group:

White Male: I think, what I'm saying is that I find the authority in this conference to be intellectualized. I find it confusing. And I find it disruptive. It doesn't allow me to really speak my mind about certain things that I do feel and think in the moment about the group. I'm trying to work it in my mind, but it's difficult. How do you clarify the authority structure and how well we're protected or not, what about safety? All those things are coming up for me.

White Male Leader: My experience of the group is that this can be a dangerous place and that your perception is that in my role as consultant I am not doing enough to protect you. So the group does not feel like a safe place, which makes it difficult to deal with the feelings in the group. The other thought I am having has to do with the managing director of the conference and your feelings about his authorization of me to take up this role. Can you authorize me to work with you? Can you authorize yourselves to do the work that you need to do here?

White Male: That makes me feel like I am waiting for permission to share.

A male group member is actively challenging the leader in this group; the challenge is being expressed on behalf of the group. Specifically, the group is challenging the authority of the white male consultant in his role as well as expressing an experience of feeling unsafe. Lack of safety in this group is symbolized by the member's reference to feeling constrained to speak openly about his feelings and also another member's reference to "waiting for permission to share" with the other members. The group consultant/leader's response is indicative of his competence to maintain the necessary task and role boundaries in the face of criticism and negative responses from the group members. In reflecting back to the members their criticism of him and their concern about the perceived lack of safety in the group, he lets them know that he has heard the group's concerns. However, in his intervention he also challenges them, by linking their feeling of safety to the larger context of the conference. He then questions their ability to fully authorize him in his role as group leader and connects that task to their need to also authorize each other to "work" in the group. The consultant/leader speaks of his role and the process of authorization for him and the members, drawing attention to the larger context of the conference in which the small group exists. He is asking the group members to consider how their lack of trust might relate to the temporary educational institution that they are in. He speaks to the challenge of the member, maintaining his role and demonstrating a capacity to adapt and work with the group and the issues that surface. He is also attempting to mobilize the group to take up its own authority to work (Heifetz, 1994).

Competencies

- *An understanding that taking up authority may include tolerating loneliness, derision, or being misunderstood*

- *The courage to speak what is felt to be unspeakable in the particular work context as long as it relates to the task of the group at hand*

- *An appreciation of the range and complexity of unconscious activity*

Leadership entails taking up an authority role that can feel isolating and lonely. The members may objectify the leader, and this behavior is indicative of their recognition that the leader's role is different from theirs. Members often test the leader's authority; they may question interventions that challenge them. It is the leaders' responsibility to manage the anxiety that may arise for the group and for self. For example, in one small study group with a female consultant/leader, there were more men than women, all from very different racial and cultural backgrounds. The consultant/leader felt that the members were discussing their differences in very simplistic ways, with the men holding court while the women listened. The group leader stated the following:

Black Female Leader: It seems that differences in this group have to be either/or, there seems to be little room to hold on to the complexity of differences in this room. You have to be antagonist, or you have to be white. Or, perhaps, being sandwiched between two white men, the way that I am right now, is a way to contain this black woman who may sound very white to many of you. Is it easier to contain than explore?

White Male:	Whaat?
	[Laughter]
White Male:	I'm sorry, it's not personal, but, what was that?
	[Laughter]
Latina Female:	You know, I'm having a real upset reaction. I've been feeling very quiet, shut down, in this group. From the beginning, I'm thinking this isn't me. And, I think, I'm often in her role. I run groups, I've been in groups. And I work on staff, and I realize this is relating to my staff, where, I say things that are very relevant, and I'm very educated, and, I watch people dismiss the value behind what I have to offer and what I have to say. And, I don't know if I'm having that reaction to you, especially because you're a man. But, when I watched you two, respond to her that way. And I realize what this is about. And it's about how hard it is, you know, and I don't think I'm the only woman in this room, I think like we've all had this experience, where, you know, you have something to offer, and you have something to say that is on point, but, what does it mean, and what's it like, when you offer up yourself to try to move something along, offer some insight, and it's just, you just reacted to like you're utterly ridiculous.

In making this type of intervention, the consultant/leader challenges the group and also speaks the unspeakable; she focuses on how the group has (consciously or unconsciously) seated her and reflects on what this might mean in relation to the discussion about differences in the group. Seating in groups is often representative of unconscious processes that are operating in the group. Thus, if all the women are seated together, or all the Latinos or Asians are seated together, the leader needs to ascertain if the seating is related to a theme or issue within the group. In this group, the consultant/leader speaks to feeling sandwiched between two white men in a conference with a theme of working with the complexity of racial-cultural differences. The two male members on each side of her are surprised by her comment, it makes them anxious, and they discard it. The Latina woman speaks about gender, as it relates to the consultant/leader's intervention, but does not speak about race. The Latina woman seems more connected to the leader's gender than race. She uses the opportunity to speak of her own feelings in the group. Her comment ultimately helped the other women from diverse races in the group engage in the conversation. The intervention challenged the group to think about unconscious meanings of its behavior and gave the Latina woman courage to articulate some feelings that may not have been revealed otherwise. By directing attention to the seating arrangement and framing what it might mean for the group, the consultant/leader's intervention provided some information that the group could then use to determine its meaning (Heifetz, 1994).

Competencies

- *The ability to reflect on and express one's internal experience rather than acting on it*

- *A respectful and curious stance toward others' learning and experience*

- *An understanding of how elements of one's own identity and history affect one's work as well as calling forth particular fantasies and projections from others in the context of groups*

Awareness of how one is feeling in one's group leadership role is essential. The group leader's feelings and emotions often run parallel to conscious and unconscious group processes and often relate to how the group is reacting to the leader. Awareness of internal processes during group sessions can help the leader avoid impulsive behavior and/or verbalizations that can adversely affect the group's process. In addition to awareness of one's internal experience in the group, it's important for leaders to also develop the skill of being able to express their feelings to the group. Disclosure of a group leader's internal experience should be done in service of the group's process and/or development. In the following example of a small study group, the members have been discussing their feelings of anxiety, discomfort, and loss due to the absence of a female member of color who failed to return to the group at the start of the session:

Black Female #1:   Well, for me, what I wanted to do was to talk about my feeling of loss, and we couldn't talk about it as long as you were waiting to start. [This comment is made to other members of the group after some tense discussion about whether to start or wait for the missing member.]

Black Female Leader: I'm struck by the fact that this group is beginning in the same way that it began in the last session. Which is that there is some confrontation, and some dialogue, about the presence, or absence, of a black woman in this room. I think that some of the dialogue is related to me. And the group's feeling about me.

Black Female #1:   Mm.

Black Female #2:   Could be. Even if you're silent, and not like a member, I presume that you are black, and you appear to me to be what I construct in my mind as black. And you have offered some very helpful interpretations, at least in my view, but you have been a little silent. So you've been here, but really not. And so, maybe some of the group's feelings, and certainly some of my feeling may be related to that. So I would agree.

Asian Male: I don't have that feeling. To be honest, I'm curious to find out, if it's only me or for you guys as well. [Checking with other members of the group]

Black Female #2:   What feeling?

Asian Member: The feeling that has something to do with the consultant being an African American woman.

Black Female Leader: I think it has something to do with me, in that it most likely has something to do with Dr. M [referring to the black female director of the conference].

In this example, as the leader of this group, it was the second author's (E.L.S.) internal experience that the group members' focus on the absent member was related to their conscious and unconscious preoccupation with her authority in the group. Her authority as group consultant/leader was intricately tied to gender, race, power, and authority, which was being enacted and discussed by the group members, as well as being a prominent theme in the conference structure. Her intervention reflected her internal experience and gave members an opportunity to reflect on whether it fit with their experience. The consultant/leader was respectful and curious about the group members' experience of her. She gave them an opportunity to speak of their experience of her and the attributes that she brought to the role. A black female member agreed with her, while an Asian male member disagreed and sought the opinions of other members. By speaking of her race and gender and that of the director of the conference, the consultant/leader is demonstrating a willingness to explore certain fantasies and projections that members might have in relation to her and the larger conference context or authority structure. Often group leaders work in the context of an agency or organization, and it is important to consider how the group is affected by the context in which it exists and works. The group is an island, held by the surrounding ocean, whether calm or turbulent.

Maintenance of a respectful and curious stance toward what group members are learning and experiencing is also reflected in the group consultant/ leader's intervention; her statement to the group allows members to reflect on and agree or disagree with what she's said, based on their own internal experience of the group process. It is important to allow members to express their feelings in reaction to the group leader's interventions. By allowing them to express their reactions to interventions, the group leader models for the members the skill of openly engaging with authority, which in turn promotes increased feelings of group safety. Heifetz (1994) points out that when there are problems in a group or organization, the members blame the authority figure(s). The openness to exploration of these feelings and concerns can help balance tension in the group.

Competency

- *The ability to recognize that individuals "carry" or express some aspect of the experience of the group as a whole, for example, scapegoating and rescuing*

Each role carries an important component of group process and development, and the emergence of each role is indicative of the group's needs, developmentally. The following excerpt is from a small study group. This example focuses on the group's continued discussion of gender, race, authority, power, and leadership. It also reveals the emergence of a scapegoated male member.

Asian Male:	But you don't have to put a name on there, there's quite a few members who've taken on a leadership role in this group.
Asian Female:	Yeah, it's not just him. It's not. It's pervasive. I've seen it in large group. I mean, I just have to go to sleep on that.
Asian Male:	That's what I'm referring to. Of being the scapegoat person, and you know, this, not all bad.
Asian Female:	I mean, it's not easy behind the scapegoat thing, you've got to talk about the issue, you know.
Asian Male:	I'm talking about the issue. . . .
Asian Female:	Instead of saying, I'm the victim, you can talk about it, the issue I mean.
Asian Male:	It's not an isolated issue; I'm not the victim. I feel offended by you, by your addressing me like that.
Asian Female:	It was not supposed to be, I mean, I'm just pointing out something. The way I felt, and it isn't just against you, but something that you had done right then, and it's not scapegoating, you know. If you'd done something outside of here, I wouldn't point you out and jump you. You know what I mean, we're talking about the issue.

Asian Male: I'm talking about the issue. The issue is to talk about leadership and differences.

Asian Female: It's not about you. That's what I'm saying [Laughs]. The issue is . . .

Black Female   I wonder what work these two members are doing on behalf
Leader: of the group, and if the men who are in the minority in this group can hold leadership roles. Perhaps that is not allowed in this group of strong women.

This group was composed primarily of black and Asian female members; there were two Asian males. The dialogue just presented is an interaction between an Asian female member and an Asian male member who had consistently challenged the views of authority of the women in the group. There was a struggle between the black and Asian women for leadership in the group. The man tried to take up a leadership role in the group as well, and all the women seemed opposed to him taking up a leadership role. He became the scapegoat in the group. The discussion and pairing of these two members represents the group's continued struggle with leadership. The male member's challenge could be viewed as the group's attempt to assert male leadership; the group's reaction to his behavior, however, is expressed by attempts to victimize and scapegoat him, thus rejecting his (e.g., male) leadership. In this instance, the male group member was able to verbalize his experience of being victimized by the group; other group members also openly acknowledged this process by making reference to him being the "scapegoat person." He goes back and forth with one of the Asian women until the consultant/leader makes an intervention that addresses the issue as one that belongs to the group and not the man or woman who has been speaking. The point of the intervention was to engage other members to own their projections and speak of their feelings. The Asian woman who confronts the Asian man could represent the strength of the gender issue over the racial-cultural differences when it came to group leadership in this group.

Projective processes of scapegoating are often not as openly acknowledged by group members as in the scenario presented. In these instances, it is the group leader's responsibility to detect and assess projective processes related to scapegoating, to provide interventions that validate what is occurring that would serve to heighten the group's awareness of their behavior, and finally, to protect the scapegoated member. Heifetz (1994) asserts that the leader has access to information that may not be available consciously to the group. In certain groups, this information is in the form of observations of verbal and nonverbal behavior in current and past group activities that can be crucial in developing insight into the group's experience. It is the leader's ability to be in the group and on the balcony simultaneously that gives access to this information.

Competencies

- *An understanding that the exercise of leadership and representation affects, and is affected by, group and intergroup dynamics*
- *An understanding of how organizational dynamics reflect the larger sociopolitical context*
- *The ability to shift one's attention to consider intrapsychic, interpersonal, group, and intergroup perspectives in order to understand what is happening in the group as a whole*

Both group and intergroup dynamics can affect a group leader's exercise of leadership. Intergroup dynamics in small groups occur between various social identity groups such as race, culture, gender, sexual orientation, age, ability/disability, and professional or organizational affiliations. Intergroup dynamics are connected to perceptions and circumstances related to power, authority, and resources in groups and institutions. The following example of a small study group session provides an example of the impact of sociopolitical context and the various levels of organizational dynamics on group-level processes:

Peter (White Male): I've never done this before. As an HIV-positive man, who finally begins to settle some issues in his own community and his place in it—it's a very rough time. I had a very rough time in the world of boys and men as a child and I come out and I come into a community of gay men where I have a equally rough time and it takes years to carve my niche and I take a positive HIV test and I'm a fucking pariah in my community. I may be doing what you're afraid is going to be done.

Perry (White Male): I really appreciate you being so honest, and I would really like to validate what I heard and it just sounds like a shitty experience. I'll just put it bluntly. You've been through a lot of shit. And what I hear you saying is that people don't acknowledge that and it fuckin' sucks and you wish that they would hear that.

Peter: Well that sucks. Oh, something in me says, "Oh shut up. It's tiresome. Who cares? You're really lucky you're alive and not sick."

Toussaint (Black Male):   But you still have pain.

Peter: I know but if I have that in me about my story, then this is what I'm talking about when I hear other people's story and part of me really does something that is just like shitty. I go, "For Christ's sake, come on. You're not like them. You're educated and you have all the earmarks of an educated person. You're articulate." Well, that's not particularly compassionate and I don't like it. But it goes off like cannon fire in me. I wrestle with it because these are not things that I like about myself. I'm sorry.

Toussaint: No problem.

Peter: I dressed with sort of unusual attention this morning and I was like, "How am I going to be a militant faggot." And I put on seven different things only to put on the thing that I was originally going to put on this morning. But there's a silent homosexual subgroup in there. Nobody's talking about it.

Leader (White Male):   Not to distract but this conference has a managing director who was very articulate about his gay identity and yet some how or another I'm not sure that was heard. And we're reeling with that information. It certainly began [as] one of the issues around this group, but I do believe there are others. And I'm also wondering whether the group is struggling with the question of what's the currency here.

Anne (White Female):   I don't understand what the word "currency" means.

Leader: What do you have to do to get in here? What do you have to suffer to get in here? I sometimes get the sense that it's a competition that is not unlike American society where who can prove their wound is bigger. Mine's bigger, I win. I will relinquish my wound to acknowledge and bow to your wound because your wound is so much bigger and its oozing and its nasty and it sticks, so you win this round— you win the competition—is what it feels like. And yet, we are at a conference to embrace differences and as does our society unfortunately revert back to one difference rather then exploring the multitude of differences. And that's not to negate the importance of the pervasiveness of the one that we seem to dwell on, but it does make the others seem less important, even though they are not.

The group member in this instance is expressing his experience of feeling isolated because of his sexual orientation; his comments reference his experiences within the group and within society, simultaneously. His comments come from his own internal experience but also seem reflective of work being done by the group-as-a-whole concerning determining what is the most valued and salient form of self-expression. This is validated by the group consultant/leader's reference to what the "currency" of group-level expression is, what type of suffering will carry the most weight, that is, be most highly valued by the group, and, most important, by the group leader. The male group member's narrative about being a gay man is also referenced by the group consultant/leader in his acknowledgment that the conference's managing director is also a gay man and the implication that the group has this information. His intervention implies that the group has unconsciously identified the "currency" as competition related to outsider status, in this instance, sexual orientation. Thus, the group consultant/leader's intervention references multiple levels of embeddedness connected to power, authority, and access to resources (e.g., at group, organizational, and institutional levels), as well as the relationship between these levels and the larger sociopolitical context. In this group, the currency of sexual orientation and the levels of disenfranchisement associated with being gay and HIV positive seemed to be an unconscious association with power and authority in the group and in the conference as a whole. The leader challenged the members to think more about who has currency and who does not have it in the group, pointing to the intergroup differences that existed among members, thus providing an opening for those who did not have currency to speak.

The issue of representation, when it comes to race, sexual orientation, and gender in relationship to authority, power, and leadership, is strong in this example. The members in the group are connecting with the authority figures through their racial identity attitudes and perceptions of what these figures represent. The managing black gay male director is seen by the members in both positive and negative associations of what it might mean for him to take up a leadership role. Members' connection with the multiple identities of the managing director, given their own fantasies, personal needs, and desires, may have little or no relevance with the director's own view of himself in role.

Competency

- *The ability to formulate group-level unconscious processes as they are occurring using words, images, analogies, and metaphors*

This competency is demonstrated in a group where the members worked quite effectively on a racial/sexual preference issue, where a white man admitted to the group that he did not find black women sexually attractive in a group with two black women (see the example in Chapter 10). The leader/ consultant was silent during the encounter, since the group was doing the work on its own. When they finished she stated, "So it seems like one of the items on the agenda for this last session is sort of truth and reconciliation." The metaphor related to the "truth and reconciliation" meetings in South Africa. The members were able to relate to this comment and continued its work in that vein. Analogies, images, and metaphors are effective ways of making a point to the group in a succinct manner. Often, group members refer to such comments for years after the group experience, indicating its impact on them and their learning. Heifetz (1994) refers to this as the leader's power to frame the group's experience in a way that makes sense and gives meaning to the experience. Some group workers are more skilled with these types of interventions than others. Group workers develop their own style over years of practice, finding a style of intervention that works for them and those they feel comfortable with.

Competencies

- *The capacity for self-containment and the ability to "hold still" emotionally long enough to identify and feel along the boundary between what resides in the group and the environment and what resides in one's self*

- *The ability to regain the consultant role after it has been lost*

- *An ability to facilitate members' application of group learning to their experiences in other contexts*

The competencies just listed involve self-containment, recognizing the difference between your feelings as a leader and those of the members, regaining role, and facilitating the application of member learning outside the group. There are times in groups when the leader will have strong feelings either about members, the group processes, or issues being discussed by the group. Learning to "hold still" and distinguish one's own feelings from those of the members can help the leader not project his or her feelings onto the group. Being able to distinguish between what resides in the group and the environment and what resides in one's self is a competency that will provide a group atmosphere of justice and fairness. Group members will also feel a sense of freedom, while at the same time staying connected. Because leaders are human, they may lose their role at some point in their work with groups. A member might make a provocative statement regarding something that the leader is very sensitive about; for example, it could be a sexist, racist, or homophobic comment. The leader might respond in a condescending or attacking manner in very much the way a member of the group would respond. In order to regain role, the leader might speak to the process of the comment and how it affected him or her. In doing this, the leader may wonder aloud to the group whether or not his or her response was a conscious or unconscious way of defending himself or herself and other members of the group. Heifetz (1994) refers to the leader's capacity to orchestrate conflict, managing the tension and creating space for negotiation and collaboration. Last, a competent leader helps members not only make sense of what they learn in the group, but also to apply their learning to contexts outside the group. For instance, a young woman who does not want to be perceived as a sexual object, but dresses in a sexually provocative manner and flirts with all the men in the group, needs to be helped to understand how her behavior and appearance may or may not coincide with her perceptions of herself. Members of the group can provide feedback, and the woman can be helped to relate her experience in the group with her experiences outside the group. It is important to consider what is gained from certain behaviors and what the pros and cons are of continuing or changing. It may be that a new perspective on behavior rather than behavioral change is most appropriate.

Summary

In this chapter, we have adapted the AKRI competencies as strategies for a broader range of groups. We have also integrated some of Heifetz's (1994) work on leadership where applicable. While groups may have members with similar demographics, each group is different, depending on the context, racial-cultural experiences, and personalities of the members. Therefore, there is no set strategy that will work for all groups. It is the leader's responsibility to assess the needs of each group, given his or her awareness and understanding of racial-cultural issues that can surface in groups, and determine the best intervention for the group in that instance. Developing competency in group work requires practice and openness to learn from the experience of self and others.

Many professionals have used the strategies discussed in this chapter successfully in their work with groups over a number of years. We have found that when there is an exploration and an understanding of feelings and thoughts, behavioral changes can occur between people, groups, and organizations. Working with groups from different racial and cultural backgrounds, attending to the differences, inquiring about their meaning, and openly discussing power differentials are strategies that allow members the opportunity to see that they are not alone. They also allow members to learn from their experiences with others who have similar and different backgrounds.

QUESTIONS FOR REVIEW AND DISCUSSION

1. List three competencies that were most helpful to you.

2. Describe a group situation in which you have or might demonstrate these competencies.

3. What would (or did) you find most challenging about using these competencies in working with groups?

4. List three competencies that might be most difficult for you.

5. Describe a group situation in which you have or might demonstrate these competencies.

6. What would (or did) you find most challenging about using these competencies in working with groups?

KEY TERMS AND CONCEPTS

AKRI competencies

Prerequisite competencies

Stage 1 and Stage 2 competencies

9

The Mature Work Group

> *The work task is like a serious parent who has his eye on intelligent planning. The basic assumptions are like fun-loving or frightened children who want immediate satisfaction of their desires. What Bion emphasizes is that both exist and that both are necessary. The basic assumption group, however, exists without effort. The work group requires all the concentration, skill, and organization of creative forces that can be mustered to bring it into full flower.*
>
> M. Rioch (1975, p. 31)

There are times in the life of a group when it is highly effective in its functioning, when members and the leader have a sense that the group can achieve its goals or task. The members and the leader experience the group as productive, unified, and capable of addressing the problems and issues before them. Working in and with such groups is the time we enjoy the most, even though the experience may only last for a short period of time. This phase of group life is often described as the working group (Corey & Corey, 2006), while others label it as the work group or the sophisticated work group (Bion, 1961). In this chapter, this phase of group life will be identified as *the mature work group,* primarily because the concepts of both of these perspectives are combined, and groups that function in this capacity demonstrate a certain amount of maturity in their behavior. The terms will be used interchangeably at times, but the term *mature work group* will be used more frequently. In our experience, when a group is working in a more mature manner, underlying dynamics continue to exist based on basic assumption functioning as described in Chapter 5. The mature work group does not exist in isolation. The mature work group and basic assumption group coexist and support one another.

Basic assumption group functioning refers to the irrational emotion-based behavior in groups that occurs when the group acts "as if" it is in a state of dependency, fight/flight, pairing, oneness, and me-ness (Bion, 1961; Lawrence, Bain, & Gould, 1996; Turquet, 1974). In psychoanalytic terms, the ego does not exist without the id or irrational aspects of the personality (Rioch, 1975). Margaret Rioch (1975) suggests that basic assumptions exist as an interference with the work group, just as primitive impulses can interfere with a mature person's functioning. In mature work groups, the basic assumptions may impede effective functioning, while at other times, the group manages to contain the anxiety created by the basic assumption sufficiently for a given amount of time in order to accomplish its task. Usually, the group is better able to manage this anxiety when members have become aware of the dynamic and how it affects their behavior and relationships in the group. We agree with Rioch:

> Man seems to be a herd animal who is often in trouble with his herd. Ineffective and self-contradictory behavior seems at times to be very common in groups—even though highly effective functioning is common at other times. (pp. 23–24)

In this chapter, the following questions are addressed: What is a mature work group? What does a mature work group look and sound like? What behaviors are inherent to the processes of the mature work group? These questions apply to the theories that have been discussed in previous chapters, especially, embedded intergroup relations theory and BART, as well as other concepts that will, it is hoped, illuminate the reader's understanding of the mature work group. The following section demonstrates and explains the chapter's concepts using an example of a mature work group.

What Is the Mature Work Group?

In the group counseling and psychotherapy literature, a working group is often defined as a stage in the group's development in which members openly share, discuss, and work on problems or concerns that are the goals of the group (Corey & Corey, 2006; Jacobs et al., 1998). In the mature work group, members are committed to exploring significant problems and have learned to pay attention to some of the dynamics that trigger anxiety in the group. During this phase of the group's work, leaders find that they are usually less active because the members have learned how to engage with each other in more productive ways. Members take on more responsibility for their behavior in the group; they initiate work more readily without waiting for the leader (Corey & Corey, 2006).

WHAT DOES A MATURE WORK GROUP LOOK AND SOUND LIKE?

A mature work group can exist for one or several sessions depending on the life span of the group on the members and the group leader. The dynamics of each group are different, and some groups work more effectively than others. Some research on work and task groups suggests that groups that are racially and culturally mixed have more difficulty working effectively with their differences (Li et al., 1999; Shaw & Barrett-Power, 1998). As stated above, the mature work group does not exist in pure form. It coexists with the basic assumption group, which may mobilize and support its functioning. There is a parallel process that occurs between the two, one representing a more intellectual task-oriented state of being, the other the emotional states of the group's anxiety, which may lead to impulsive, acting-out behavior. According to Rioch (1975), for effective group functioning, the basic assumptions "must be subservient to and used in the service of the work task. They make good servants and poor masters" (p. 30). A group of elementary school students depending on their teacher to take them to the park is an example of when the basic assumption group is being mobilized to support the work group. The students' dependency on the teacher allows them to line up, hold hands, follow prediscussed rules, and so forth. Similarly, our experience of conducting groups in hospital settings has revealed a pattern of dependency that patients have on hospital staff that often fosters effective functioning of patient care procedures. When conducting a group of veterans with spinal cord injuries, the first author (M.B.M.) found that when patients accepted a certain level of dependency after injury, they were able to develop a sense of independence in terms of individual and group capabilities. In their case, dependence, interdependence, and independence coexisted as a difficult reality of the present situation; working within this context rather than in a state of denial enhanced more productive rehabilitation.

CHARACTERISTICS OF A MATURE WORK GROUP

The following is a list of some characteristics of the mature work group along with the basic assumptions that could affect effective functioning. We invite the reader to think of groups that the reader has either been in or observed, add to the list what the reader thinks is appropriate, and then think about how these characteristics apply (see Table 9.1). Doing this may help the reader better understand the groups' functioning.

TABLE 9.1 Characteristics of a Mature Work Group	
Mature Work Group	*Basic Assumption Group*
Members work to achieve the *task* or *goal* of the group.	Members either *fight* against or take *flight* (Bion, 1961) from working on the task. They might engage in a fight among themselves or challenge the leader, or they might talk about matters totally external to the group, denying whatever issues confront them.
Members develop a sense of *trust* in the group and the leader and feel comfortable sharing certain aspects of self. The group environment feels safe enough to take personal risks. Members from different racial and cultural groups openly share feelings and thoughts about each other and work to understand rather than debate opposing values and worldviews.	Members do not trust each other and continuously feel vulnerable to possible threat or danger in the group. Members may be stuck in *me-ness* (Lawrence et al., 1996), fear of loss of self, and engulfment. Members may fear exposure to racism, ethnocentricity, classism, sexism, homophobia, and the repercussions of their values and beliefs in the context of their social identity group affiliation. Member differences in ideological beliefs, racial and cultural values, and personalities all affect the development of trust in the group. Differences can create conflict or *fight/flight* (Bion, 1961) behaviors in groups. Members struggle and seem unable to resolve differences.
A sense of *inclusion* among members indicates a sense of belonging to the group and a valuing of what each member has to contribute to the group. There is a capacity to recognize the racial-cultural contexts in the realm of the larger society and the world.	Members form subgroups based on professional, educational, ideological, and social identities, where allegiance to the subgroup is stronger than to the group-as-a-whole. Member personalities also create concerns for inclusion when one member is shy or silent, while others are more active. Members may feel a sense of *dependency* (Bion, 1961) on the leader and other members of the group to help them feel included. A sense of *one-ness* (Turquet, 1974) may also exist for members who have a strong need to belong to the group.
The members work with *conflict* that surfaces in the group. Different perspectives are discussed and accepted by members. Members might at times agree to disagree and move on rather than continue the conflict, drawing boundaries for future work to be done.	Members get stuck with conflict. There may be two or more opposing camps in the conflict, none willing to understand the other's perspective, each blaming the other for the stalemate. This could be a *fight/flight* (Bion, 1961) defensive mode to manage the group's anxiety about the potential threat of the conflict to the group. Sometimes conflict in groups is related to group member's wishes to remain in but not a part of the group, representing a sense of *me-ness* (Lawrence et al., 1996).

Mature Work Group	Basic Assumption Group
Confrontation takes place in the group in a productive and respectful manner. Members have a sense that they are being confronted about certain behaviors to enhance their learning. They do not experience the confrontation as an attack on them personally.	Confrontation is experienced as a personal attack, members feel vulnerable. Talk about racial-cultural differences creates divisive gaps of unspeakable issues due to fear of exposure of racism among members. Members often will take *flight* from such confrontation, leaving a heavy or tense feeling in the air, present but seemingly unworkable.
Members experience a *willingness to take risks* by sharing uncomfortable information, behaving in new ways, or taking up different roles in a group. Members take risks and learn that they can survive and even be supported by group members.	Members fear taking risks and the group environment may not feel safe enough for certain members. This can happen when an African American, Asian, Latina/Latino, American Indian, Eastern Indian, or Caucasian member finds himself or herself the only one or perhaps two or three in a group that are predominantly of a different racial-cultural group, and the group leader belongs to the predominant group. Fear often takes the form of *fight/flight* (Bion, 1961) behavior in groups. Members fight with each other or the leader, or they take flight by focusing on something outside the group.
Recognition and acknowledgment of differences and similarities among members and a willingness to work with rather than against their existence in the group. This could be a healthy sense of *dependency and interdependency* on the talents of the diverse members in the group.	Members deny the importance of differences in the group. There is a pull for a *one-ness* (Turquet, 1974) in the group. There may be a fear of dependency needs of group members, making it harder to acknowledge desires for belonging to the group.
Members take time for *reflection and self-examination of roles* and interactions in the group. They share their reflections with members for feedback. They inquire about others' perception of them and the roles they take up in the group.	Members do not feel safe sharing their reflections in the group. They may state that they are learning little or nothing in the group. Members may choose to *fight* with the leader or members rather than discuss feelings about their role in the group and others' perception of them.

SOURCE: Bion (1961); Corey and Corey (2006); Lawrence et al. (1996); Turquet (1974); Yalom (1995).

AN EXAMPLE OF A MATURE WORK GROUP

The following example is drawn from a small study group in a group relations conference. It was a diverse group—racially, culturally, and professionally.
There were 12 members who were self-selected to be videotaped for an educational video. It was one of the six small study groups that were formed to work
with a consultant for four sessions during a weekend nonresidential conference. The group consists of two black women: Margaret (an experienced mental health professional) and Monica (an undergraduate student). Other group
members included one black man, Neil (also an undergraduate student); two
Asians, Lee (a male graduate student) and Agnes (a young professional woman);
two white women (both graduate students), Margo (a Ukrainian immigrant)
and Kim (a Jewish American); and five white men, James, Patrick, and John
(all three professionals) and Andrew and Greg (two graduate students). This is
the fourth and last session of the group. During the first session, James, one
of the professionals, had talked about the group consultant, a black woman, as
the beautiful member of the female consultant team. The consultant, an African
American, is a tall, attractive, light-tan-complexioned woman, with long curly
hair. During another event of the conference where the members form small
groups that work alone, consultants were only made available at the request of
the group. The group that James had joined worked on the topic of sexuality.
The group created an exercise that involved sharing and writing down on small
pieces of paper thoughts and feelings about sexual preferences that were usually
unspeakable in groups and organizations. He told the group that he woke up at
5:30 that morning in a state of panic about what he had shared. He said that he
was not sexually attracted to black women. He feared that the rest of the
conference would be "lightning bolts and thunder" for him. There were two black
women in this small group. The designated consultant to the group was a
black woman with whom he had flirted during the first session, and the director and associate director of the conference were black women:

James: There is something I said the first day, which is connected, to our
         sexuality group that four of us here belong to. I admitted that I
         don't have sexual attractions to black women. That came out in the
         conference that I feel like was a . . . . I'm scared shitless when I real-
         ized at 5:30 this morning. There were no black women in the sex-
         uality group. They're [black women] excluded from my sexual
         fantasy life. Well, yeah, I made this comment about how beautiful
         our African American consultant was in here. And I feel like—I
         mean afterwards in our sexuality group I got, it was lightning bolts
         and thunder and I feel like the rest of the conference is going to be
         lightning bolts and thunder about what I said.

Monica: Well, I feel like you are attracted to black women, but because of the fact that you identified our consultant as beautiful. So I think that's what's really scaring you right now is that "I don't in my mind think that I should be attracted to black women," but the fantasy is and the deeper thought is, "I really do," and I think that's what's scaring you right now is that you really do. You're coming to that realization.

James: I'm totally willing to note that I experienced both our consultant and several of the consultants and members who are African American women as beautiful and dignified and brilliant and wise and have rocked my world. But when I think about who I want to get in bed with, who I want to undress, I think about white women.

Margaret: Okay. Okay. The attraction. Okay. I'm thinking attraction. Okay.

James: Attraction definitely, rocked my world, and I find that beautiful, moving, and powerful.

Margaret: Okay.

James: But I have this bias at a deeper level. It's a bias that I hold that I felt like was reflective of the membership of our sexuality group that had no African American women.

Margaret: What had been your fantasy as to what would happen to you about having to share it?

James: At first when the sexuality group reconvened, it was the first thing that was said. That was the one I couldn't own. All the other secrets we kind of came to together, and we realized that they wouldn't all be our secrets, but we would come and say, "We're the group that sort of talked about the unspoken." And of all the unspoken things, one member of our group said, my comment was the most difficult to take in. That is when I wanted to climb into a hole.

Margaret: Why is that?

James: Well, what she said. When I heard that, I was like, "Oh, God." I'd been battling all morning inside myself about whether to say, whether to write that one down on a little slip of paper, and I was like if my own group member or someone who I felt all this trust with for 6 hours about all these deep sort of feelings, if the people who we had that much trust with couldn't take it, the rest of the conference is really not going to take it.

Margaret: I'm not sure . . . I do not understand what it is that you're so shameful about.

James: I feel like it's the most complete unrepentant racial bias. I mean I feel like in our libidinal life, we have biases that are kind of unconscious, and I don't feel like I'm a raving racist because of it. But it's not something that—it feels icky. It feels ugly.

Monica: I don't think you should feel like that. I think it's just what your preference is. My sexual preference, when I think about who I want to have sex with. I don't really want to have sex with a skinny man. That's just me.

[Laughter]

James: Well I guess that excludes me then. [James is tall and slim]

Monica: I don't think that you should feel ashamed of that. I think you should just embrace it as, "This is my own personal preference." There are other preferences that I have that I don't feel ashamed of because it's not just a race issue or my own bias. So I don't think you should feel ashamed, because I wasn't offended. I don't know about Margaret, but I wasn't offended.

Margaret: Well, Monica, I am truly pleased to be here with you. My thought is that what I want is respect and appreciation of me as a person. I mean I have no interest in being a part of your sexual fantasies, so if you feel that the idea of being a racist is about what your private sexual fantasies are about, that's not it for me. I'm much more interested in hearing about your respect of difference and your willingness to recognize that I have talents and skills and strengths that are equal. The other thing is that I was thinking about you, and I felt that I wanted you to know that your sharing of a personal story in the RAG (Review and Application Group) helped me to be less pissed off with you because our initial interaction was about your being disrespectful to me. And I held onto that. And so my hearing your personal struggle helped me to recognize that sometimes when I have immediate interactions with somebody that is disrespectful that it takes energy, my emotional energy, that I need to be able to figure out how to get my emotional energy back and not to hold on to what it is that I would refer to as a subtle indignity that happens with me often in terms of the race stuff and white men. And when I heard you talking here about your pain and struggle that melted for me. And so, if indeed, the only issue is that you have that's biased is your sexual fantasy then surely you don't have a problem with me.

James: In the here and now, your two comments, you both have been great; in particular, you have been very powerful in my mind, in my thoughts about this conference. My respect for you and my respect for you giving me a hard time at times have been great. I also respect you for talking about this. Your helping me through my change feels really great. I appreciate it.

Andrew: I feel like we're finally being able to talk about our power and authority. I mean what I heard from you is like this is—your sexual fantasy doesn't make me feel like a person in your life. It's about your showing respect for my abilities. And then you totally empowered him to feel okay with his thoughts. I just think that's great, this feeling all of a sudden. We're finally talking about this stuff.

Neil: Well, I have a feeling of just like someone being so honest within the group—like I know we've all been kind of honest, but someone revealing really tough things to the group, and the group being a support system for that. Mary and Monique were being a support system for you. And I feel like we haven't had that until just now.

In this example of a mature work group, there are a number of characteristics to be noted. First, one of the tasks of the group was to study its own behavior, especially behavior related to power and authority in groups and organizations. In this example, members discussed racial dynamics related to issues of power and authority. There is potential for intergroup conflict, between the black and white members and between women and men. The boundaries of the group seem clear; members are committed to the group and have developed cohesiveness. The members seem less interested in the authority structure and more in their own functioning. Members have developed sufficient trust for James to share his feelings of shame for having a racial bias or sexual preference. The issues in this group are inclusion, confrontation, conflict, willingness to take risks, and acknowledgment of differences.

James confesses that he does not include black women in his intimate life. This confession could have easily caused the group to feel anxious and moved them into basic assumption fight/flight behavior. Initially, Monica's comment that perhaps unconsciously he was attracted to black women could have increased group anxiety, causing members to begin discussing situations outside the group. It could have also been a pull for dependency on the female consultant to protect the black female members. Or the group might depend on the consultant to protect James from his fear of being ostracized by the group and labeled as a racist. Monica also confronts James concerning his owning his sexual preference. Rather than take flight from this confrontation,

James stays with the group by owning his experience. The two black women worked to help James feel accepted with his sexual preference of a racial intimate partner. Margaret stated that she wanted to be respected and treated equally, while Monica assured him of the right to his sexual preference. When James refutes her interpretation of his secret attraction to black women, she looks at him and announces her preference for men of larger frame, possibly to let him know how it feels to be excluded. She challenges him and acknowledges and accepts their differences without taking flight from the issue being discussed. That James is willing to take the risk of being labeled as having a racial bias in the context of this particular temporary institution is indicative of a level of trust that he experienced in the group as a safe enough container. In this group, members and the leader were able to contain the anxiety that surfaced around racial bias long enough to discuss and process what was occurring.

Strategies for Assisting the Mature Work Group

The reader may notice that there was no intervention made by the group consultant in the previous example. The group consultant's silence was indicative of working to empower the group to work more efficiently and independently. Earlier in this session, one member had stated that the group felt like a sanctuary to him. The consultant asked the group, "So if this is a sanctuary, what kind of work gets done? What gets sacrificed?" Perhaps her questions allowed James to speak about his fears. Perhaps, he was also putting himself up to be sacrificed for having a racial bias. The group could then have worked to crucify him. However, instead of doing that it worked to save and join with him. The two black women did not personify the "angry black woman" who is so often stereotypically portrayed; they were calm and actively engaged with James. The black woman consultant did not appear to be upset; she stayed with the group, working in a nonjudgmental manner. Group members managed differences that could potentially have created intergroup conflict. Once this part of the discussion seemed resolved, the leader intervened by saying, "So it seems like one of the items on the agenda for this last session is sort of truth and reconciliation." Her metaphor captured the work of the group and allowed them to move on to another issue. Another member then began to talk about her feelings of discomfort of being in the group with someone who was a teaching assistant in a course she was taking. These two members along with the help of other members explored what this experience had been like for them.

Strategies for working with the mature work group are staying with the group and interpreting processes while simultaneously leaving room for the members to do their work. When the mature work group engages in confrontations, the leader does not need to step in quickly to protect members. A member of the group will take up this role. The group is in this phase, in part, because of the work that the leader has done to assist them in getting there. Thus, the leader needs to trust that the group is capable of doing more work on its own at this stage of its development. When the mature work group is having difficulty, especially when working with differences, the leader can help members in a number of ways. Holvina (2004) suggests that members can be asked to inquire about each others' thoughts and feelings. Members can be invited to disclose their own feelings rather than ask others to do so. Members can encourage each other to ask difficult questions, to make differences explicit and show support while doing so, and to seek common ground. In the previous example, the members were inquiring about James's feelings and thoughts; he was able to disclose how he felt. James and Margaret asked difficult questions, and James did not take Monica's comment about his possible attraction to black women as an escape from his anxiety. He instead made the differences explicit and found that Monica and others were still supportive. The basic assumptions of fight/flight and dependency were mobilized to work through the anxiety rather than escape from it.

During the phase when the mature work group exists, the leader needs to keep in mind the basic assumptions that have been operating in the group and ways in which they can be used to continue to mobilize the group productively, as well as to impede the group's functioning. Containment of anxiety in the group is important, but if the leader works harder than the members on containment, it suggests that the members are not capable of holding the group. Thus, the leader's extra work is often a signal of the leader's anxiety and not the group's. The trust of the leader in the group's capacity to work at a mature level is similar to a parent trusting that her or his child can walk without needing assistance. If the child stumbles, she or he is capable of getting herself or himself up and continuing to walk. The dilemma is to understand when to and when not to offer assistance. Resolving this dilemma for the group depends on the leader—what the leader knows about the group members and how the leader applies the theoretical concepts to assist the members in their work.

Outcomes of the Mature Work Group

The mature work group leads to change and transformation in the lives of those who participate. Those who have been members of successful group experiences report that they have gained new perspectives on people and issues and have learned about the roles they tend to take up in groups and how they should work with authority and authorization of others in roles. Yalom (1995) identified a number of therapeutic factors that occur in groups: caring and acceptance, group cohesiveness, universality, imparting information, feedback, interpersonal learning, catharsis, hope, and corrective emotional experience. A brief description of each of these concepts follows:

- *Caring and acceptance:* Members demonstrate caring by listening to and by their involvement in the groups that can be expressed in the form of conflict and confrontation, as well as tenderness and compassion for others in the group (Corey & Corey, 2006). Acceptance is demonstrated in the support that is given to members, especially when they are struggling with disclosure or taking a risk in the group.

- *Group cohesion:* The group is cohesive when members experience a sense of belonging, acceptance, and support in the group, even when they are saying things that others may not agree with. Members look out for one another and are concerned about each other's well-being. The group has an identity and members value being a part of the group.

- *Universality:* Members learn that they are not alone, that others have similar concerns and share their feelings. Members learn that although they are different, they have similar feelings and experiences. A woman who is recently divorced and feeling frustrated about dating again learns that two younger women are having similar problems. A Latino man who is angry about having had to change his name so that a priest in the United States could more easily pronounce it learns that other Latinos and other immigrants have had similar experiences.

- *Imparting information:* This is the cognitive component of learning in groups. Members obtain information from other members that are useful in their lives. When members engage in the process of clarification, interpretation, explanation, the formulation of ideas, and hearing alternative perspectives on a problem, they learn a different cognitive framework from which to view their problem (Corey & Corey, 2006). Information obtained from members can, at times, be more valuable than information from the group leader.

- *Feedback and interpersonal learning:* Interpersonal learning takes place through feedback from others. When feedback is genuine and given sensitively, it can have a huge impact on interpersonal learning. In the previous example, when Margaret tells James that she was no longer "pissed off" at him after hearing about his personal struggle, she is giving feedback and letting him know that she could identify with his pain. She shares that she has learned something about herself and how she manages issues of race with white men.

- *Catharsis:* The freedom to ventilate feelings in a safe or nonthreatening environment with other people can be therapeutic. Expressing intense feelings of anger or joy that have been bottled inside for too long a period is liberating for the spirit and soul. Although having a cathartic experience is very good for some members, it may not be for all. Some members may feel a sense of shame after expressing certain negative feelings about their family. For example, a young Asian woman may state that she is angry with her father because he refuses to allow her to date a young man she is attracted to. If she is more traditional in her beliefs, she may feel that it was inappropriate for her to reveal this type of information about her father, leaving her with a feeling of shame.

• *Hope:* "Hope is the belief that change is possible" (Corey & Corey, 2006, p. 210). Hope is crucial in groups because it is a belief that life can be better, that things can change. Without hope, there is little growth and development of the group. Hope is usually demonstrated in the stories that different members tell and the leader's ability to assist members in reframing negative perspectives to include hopeful possibilities. For example, the leader in the above group commented about the group's work on truth and reconciliation. She was pointing out the group's work around hope that they could resolve and work out differences in the group.

• *Corrective emotional experience:* A corrective emotional experience involves exposure to a similar experience that the member has had in the past but under circumstances that can bring about a more positive experience. In groups, there is the opportunity to experience different types of tensions: competition, sibling rivalry, struggles for dominant status, sexual tensions, and racial-cultural differences (Yalom, 1995). When the group feels safe and supportive, these differences can emerge and members can receive feedback and some reality testing. James learned that the black women were more interested in his respect for them than his sexual preferences. His fears of being labeled became more complex. For instance, he began to wonder if his sexual preference for white women could be generalized to racial bias against black women or all black people, or was it simply a preference as identified by Monica?

Summary

In this chapter, we have discussed the mature work group, providing characteristics, an example, and strategies to work with a group in this phase. The mature work group coexists with the basic assumption group. The mature work group is able to mobilize and/or contain basic assumption behaviors for effective functioning. The basic assumption group needs to function in the service of the mature work group.

The chapter concludes with a review of Yalom's (1995) therapeutic factors and some examples for further clarification.

QUESTIONS FOR REVIEW AND DISCUSSION

1. Describe a mature work group. What does it look like? What does it sound like?

2. Consider a group that you have been a part of and note the aspects that made the group a work group and the basic assumptions that interfered with work group functioning.

3. What are the therapeutic outcomes of a mature work group?

KEY TERMS AND CONCEPTS

Basic assumption group

Caring and acceptance

Catharsis

Corrective emotional experience

Feedback and interpersonal learning

Group cohesion

Hope

Imparting information

Mature work group

Mature work group outcomes

Strategies for working with the mature work group

Universality

MATURE WORK GROUP ASSESSMENT FORM

Use the assessment form to determine whether a group you have observed or participated in was in a mature work group phase. Consider the basic assumptions that interfered with work group functioning.

GROUP DEMOGRAPHICS

Type and task of group: _____

_____

Number of group members: _____

Number of female group members: _____

Number of male group members: _____

Racial-cultural composition of all group members:_____

Provide a brief description of the mature work group functioning: _____

_____

_____

_____

BASIC ASSUMPTION FUNCTIONING

Describe the group's basic assumption behavior. List the basic assumptions that occurred:

_____

_____

_____

_____

Describe interventions that were made regarding the group's basic assumption behavior:

_____

_____

_____

_____

_____

Describe interventions that were made regarding racial-cultural dynamics and basic assumption behavior:

_____

_____

_____

_____

10

Termination

Termination in groups can be viewed in two ways. There is the termination of each session and the termination of the group's work together. In our work as professors and group consultants, we consider the termination of each session to be a form of modeling for the ending of the group. The ending of each session requires a group worker to have the skills for setting boundaries of time, task, and territory, as well as guidelines for the group to be aware that the group sessions begin and end at a certain time and place. Consistent adherence to this establishes a strong foundational structure for the group to work and attend to the completion of its tasks. It is essential that a group leader discuss the life of the group so that those who participate are clear about expectations. Group leaders must also develop heightened awareness of their own feelings and attitudes about termination to facilitate productive group termination (Corey & Corey, 2006). In this last chapter, we address the issue of termination in groups, keeping in mind that when members come from different racial and cultural backgrounds, cultural values may influence the ways in which members think about and experience endings. We will discuss managing issues of separation in the context of member differences, noting the importance of considering personal and cultural values that may affect the ending of relationships. We believe that the ending of a group is a metaphor for the many endings of life's short- and long-term relationships.

A Reflective Time

The termination phase of the group is a time for members to reflect on what they have learned about themselves in groups and about group functioning in general. The purpose of the closing sessions of a group is to provide some time to summarize and highlight group member experiences, assess the growth and changes that have occurred during the life of the group, check for unfinished business, provide feedback, and learn more about managing good-byes or separation (Jacobs et al., 1998). Members, for example, may reflect on what they have learned about managing time and emotional boundaries, relationships with authority figures, the role they tend to take up in groups, and how it affects relationships. Members have had an opportunity to experience the ways in which the group managed their boundaries and the various roles that members take up in group, including their own valence for a particular role; they have learned when the group is on and off task and some of the consequences of this behavior. Some groups are more able to verbalize their learning than others; it is the group leader's responsibility to help and encourage the members to identify their learning in concrete, specific terms. We caution group leaders to allow the members to voice their learning before offering their own. We have found that sometimes group leaders underestimate the power and depth of learning that a group has experienced. For instance, members who seem to have gotten little from the group may report, at termination, significant experiences that have affected their processes of learning.

The traditional format that is offered in most group texts suggests that the group leader needs to be cognizant of the task of consolidating member learning (Corey & Corey, 2006). The leader can state that as the group comes to an end, there may be feelings or thoughts that some members have been holding on to, that there might be unfinished business, and this would be a time to discuss it, so that they do not carry the sense of a missed opportunity with them. The leader can also facilitate member feedback, by helping members speak about their experience and providing examples of behaviors or interactions for clarity and understanding. This can be done by helping members review what they have learned, providing opportunities for giving and receiving feedback, applying learning in a group to outside situations, and conducting an evaluation and possibly some follow-up of member learning. This is an important process for termination and one that certainly needs to be kept in mind by group leaders.

AMBIVALENT FEELINGS ABOUT TERMINATION

The ambivalent feelings that most members and leaders experience during termination are an integral part of the termination process (LaFarge, 1990). These ambivalent feelings relate to culturally different ways of endings. According to LaFarge (1990), at the termination of the group there are two sets of conflicting feelings: (1) grief and relief and (2) resolution and dissonance. Grief can be experienced in both positive and negative ways. Group members can mourn with a focus on the positive or negative aspects of the group's life, usually expressed as missed opportunities to work interpersonal issues. Relief can be experienced as an acknowledgment of the struggles, stresses, and pains of group life and the peace of mind of not having to focus on group dynamics on a regular basis. Thus, termination can signify a release from the necessity of expending time and energy to work on difficult relationships and issues. Feelings of relief, however, can be difficult for group members to express because such expressions can be viewed as lack of a desire to "continue working to create a perfect group," as well as a wish for the termination of the group's life, as opposed to mourning the group's ending (p. 177).

Resolution during group termination implies that the group has been able to resolve problems or difficult relations between members. Members may seek to reduce the differences between them, include members who have been ostracized or scapegoated, and achieve a sense of oneness in the group (LaFarge, 1990). For some groups, resolution may be experienced as a loss of individuality for the members, which is similar to their experiences of joining the group. Fears of being swallowed up by the group can push some members to struggle with dissonance in order to maintain individuality. Dissonance can be manifested in members' anger and by silence.

PREMATURE TERMINATION

Termination by members of a group can occur prematurely. One form of premature termination can occur when one or more group members simply stops attending group sessions at the beginning or middle phases of the group's life. Research conducted about cultural issues concerning early termination in counseling has hypothesized that minority group individuals may terminate the therapeutic relationship because of experiences of bias. Clients may feel that the therapeutic services that are provided are incongruent or inappropriate with their life experiences, culturally (Sue & Sue, 2008). In instances of premature termination of group members, it is important for the group leader to conduct a follow-up inquiry with the client in order to acquire information about the client's premature termination. It is also important for the group leader to reassess her or his level of cultural competence, as well as any group dynamics that may have precipitated the client's termination from the group.

A second type of premature termination is more related to basic assumption functioning and avoidance of completion of the group's task and concerns members' ambivalence or anxiety about separation. In these instances, the focus on termination is usually characterized by members expressing a desire for the ending of the group; for example, they may talk about what they will do after the group ends and/or how relieved they will be when the group ends. Members may negate the importance of the group's task by focusing on termination, by stating the futility of the work the group has been doing. Cultural attitudes about ending may influence this type of group behavior. In these instances, it is important for the group leader to recognize that these expressions symbolize the group's struggles with managing conscious and unconscious anxieties concerning survival and termination. Acknowledgment of ambivalent feelings about the group can usually be related to experiences outside the group, where some members may have a difficult time. It could be an opportunity for the leader to integrate some early observations of a member or members with how they are managing termination in the group.

CULTURAL VALUES AND TERMINATION

The ways in which members and the leader deal with the emotions related to ending is influenced by group norms, personality, and cultural values. Each group member and the leader have grown up in a family or community system that has oriented them to certain cultural ways of ending relationships. Group leaders need to be cognizant of the different ways in which members may choose to deal with termination that are related to their cultural values. A model for understanding the cultural values of different groups developed by Kluckhohn and Strodtbeck (1961) is useful in considering the ways in which members from different racial and cultural backgrounds might deal with termination in groups. They provide five different areas of relationship dimensions:

1. *People to nature/environment:* mastery or harmony

2. *Time orientation:* past, present, future

3. *People relations:* lineal, individual, collective

4. *Mode of activity:* doing, being, becoming

5. *Human nature:* good or bad

Next, we consider each of these areas of relationships with reference to LaFarge's (1990) work concerning ambivalent feelings about group termination.

People to Nature/Environment

This cultural value involves a sense of mastery over one's environment or a sense of harmony with it. An individual with Western values may experience the grief of termination as a missed opportunity to master or achieve certain relationships with other members or to successfully resolve certain issues. Members with Eastern or non-Western cultural values may experience the termination as relief from confronting issues that members are not yet ready to deal with. Their sense of timing for resolving issues may be more in harmony with nature, which operates on a time frame that is not determined by humans. Some members may view time as a part of the cure, manifesting change, patience, strong spiritual beliefs, and faith in the harmony of the universe, which will help resolve problems; beginnings and endings are a part of the cycle of life.

Time Orientation

People from different cultural backgrounds have different orientations to time. Americans tend to be more oriented toward the future (Kluckhohn & Strodtbeck, 1961), while those from other countries may be more present- or past-oriented. Group members who have cultural values that are more oriented to the past may need to spend more time reflecting on what has happened in the group's life, or they may prefer to focus on group experiences that have occurred in the past, whereas those who are more individually focused may want to discuss their individual learning. Some members will be more verbal about their feelings and what they have learned, while others may not feel comfortable discussing unpleasant experiences or feelings that they have had in the group. The leader could consider having members provide written reactions to their experience in the group.

People Relations

Some societies are more individually oriented, while others are collective. The United States can be characterized as an individually oriented society since it is known for its focus on individual responsibility, achievement, independence, and autonomy (Sue & Sue, 2008), while Japan is characterized as collectively oriented with an emphasis on the family and community as being responsible for each other and on interdependence in relationships. Group members who are more individually oriented may focus on the self and what they have gained, while those from collective societies will tend to focus on the group. Members who are more individually oriented might feel more disappointment or unhappiness about personal missed opportunities in the group, while those who have a collective orientation might grieve over what the group did not achieve or what they did not contribute to the group's learning. Those who are individually oriented might be comfortable with their ability to feel a sense of resolve for certain issues in the group, while others might only be comfortable with processing the group's resolution. The leader might consider checking with members about unfinished business. Members who are not comfortable verbalizing their feelings could be encouraged to write them down and give them to the leader the week before. The leader can find ways to discuss the comments as broader issues for the group rather than focusing on the individuals.

Activity

There are two activity dimensions, doing and being-in-becoming. White U.S. cultural values are centered on doing, taking action, managing the situation at hand, while other populations, such as the American Indians and Latinos, prefer a being or being-in-becoming mode of activity (Sue & Sue, 2008). Doing or taking action is associated with taking control of the situation, while being-in-becoming is more inner and spiritually focused. Group members who tend to be more in the doing dimension may be pulled to take action in resolving problems the group has experienced, while those who are more being-in-becoming may feel that things will work out over time and that each member will grow to understand as he or she reflects on the group's experience. For these individuals, there may not be a pull to resolve the problem before the group ends. As stated above, some members may be drawn to discuss unfinished business in a direct manner, while others will feel less comfortable with this approach. For groups that have been meeting for some time, the leader will have developed some understanding of the personality and cultural backgrounds of the members, which can be valuable when helping them work with termination issues.

Human Nature

Some societies perceive humans as inherently good, bad, mixed, or neutral. For example, an individual who believes that humans are by nature good will experience group members as good and will expect that they will be kind in giving and receiving feedback during the termination phase. Individuals who believe that humans are bad or evil may be more cautious in giving feedback for fear of what they might get in return for their honesty. Finally, individuals who have mixed feelings and are neutral may be more open to the possibilities that members are products of their environment and could behave in either good and or bad ways.

Recognition and understanding of cultural values and how they affect the life of the group and termination for members is crucial in racially and culturally mixed groups. We consider this a time when the leader has an opportunity to integrate a series of observations of members and the group in order to foster termination of the group in a productive manner. Leaders are advised that termination is a time of transition for members. If it is a counseling or psychotherapy group that has existed for a year or more, members will need more time to process termination; if it is a task group that came together around a specific goal, it is understood by the members that the life of the group is related to the completion of the task; if it is a psychoeducational group, members will have been told about the number of sessions during orientation. Whatever the type of group, members develop relationships that require acknowledgment and some time to make meaning of their experience. Evaluations of the group experience can be very helpful feedback for the leader in understanding what members liked and did not like about their experience and in providing important information for planning future groups. A brief questionnaire that members could fill out anonymously at the last session can have questions such as the following:

- What was your most valuable learning experience in the group?
- What do you wish could have happened in the group that did not?
- What would you like to have been done differently?
- What members influenced you the most?

Leaders could also consider doing follow-up sessions with individual members a month after termination in order to see how they are doing and if they have any reflections about their experience in the group that they would like to share.

Summary

In this chapter, we briefly addressed the various issues that groups encounter during termination. Leaders are responsible for helping the group reflect on its experience, provide opportunities for feedback, and work on unresolved issues that linger in the group. Given the time frame for termination, some issues may be left unresolved, and this is a microcosm of group experiences in daily life. The termination phase is also filled with members' ambivalent feelings about the group, which may be characterized by expressions of grief and relief and resolution and dissonance. Premature termination may occur when members stop attending group sessions or when members avoid completion of the group task by an excessive focus on termination. Members' cultural values influence how they manage the group termination.

QUESTIONS FOR REVIEW AND DISCUSSION

1. What are the ambivalent feelings that many members might experience at the end of the group?

2. What are the cultural values that might influence the ways in which members manage termination?

3. Describe a situation in a group you have observed where your cultural values influenced the manner in which members dealt with termination of the group.

4. What are your attitudes and feelings about ending relationships? What cultural values can you identify that affect your attitudes and feelings about termination?

KEY TERMS AND CONCEPTS

Human nature   People to nature/environment
Mode of activity   Time orientation
People relations

References

A. K. Rice Institute for the Study of Social Systems. (2003). *Group relations consultant competencies*. Retrieved May 13, 2009, from http://www.akriceinstitute.org

Alderfer, C., & David, A. (1988). The significance of race and ethnicity for understanding organizational behavior. In C. Cooper & I. T. Robertson (Eds.), *International review of industrial and organizational psychology* (pp. 1–41). Oxford, UK: Wiley.

Alderfer, C. P. (1977). Improving organizational communication through long-term intergroup intervention. *Journal of Applied Behavioral Science, 13*(2), 193–210.

Alderfer, C. P. (1994). A white man's perspective of the unconscious processes within black-white relations in the United States. In E. J. Trickett, R. J. Watts, & D. Birman (Eds.), *Human diversity: Perspectives on people in context* (pp. 201–229). San Francisco: Jossey-Bass.

Alderfer, C. P. (1997). Embedded intergroup relations and racial identity development theory. In C. E. Thompson & R. T. Carter (Eds.), *Racial identity theory: Applications to individual, group, and organizational interventions* (pp. 237–263). Mahwah, NJ: Lawrence Erlbaum.

Alderfer, C. P., & Smith, K. (1982). Studying intergroup relations embedded in organizations. *Administrative Science Quarterly, 27,* 35–65.

American Counseling Association. (1995). *Code of ethics and standards of practice.* Alexandria, VA: Author.

American Psychological Association. (1993). Guidelines for providers of psychological services to ethnic, linguistic, and culturally diverse populations. *American Psychologist, 48*(1), 45–48.

American Psychological Association. (2002). Ethical principles of psychologists and code of conduct. *American Psychologist, 57*(12), 1060–1073.

Arce, C. A. (1981). A reconsideration of Chicano culture and identity. *Daedalus, 110,* 177–192.

Association for Specialists in Group Work. (2000a). Best practices guidelines. *The Group Worker, 29*(Suppl. 3), 1–5.

Association for Specialists in Group Work. (2000b). Principles for diversity: Competent group workers. *Journal for Specialists in Group Work, 24*(1), 7–14.

Atkinson, D. R., Morten, G., & Sue, D. W. (1989). A minority identity development model. In D. R. Atkinson, G. Morten, & D. W. Sue (Eds.), *Counseling American minorities* (pp. 35–52). Dubuque, IA: W. C. Brown.

Bales, R. F., & Strodtbeck, F. L. (1951). Phases in group problem solving. *Journal of Abnormal and Social Psychology, 46,* 485–495.

Bennis, W. G., & Shepard, H. A. (1974). A theory of group development. In G. S. Gibbard, J. J. Hartmann, & R. D. Mann (Eds.), *Analysis of groups* (pp. 127–153). San Francisco: Jossey-Bass.

Berg, D., & Smith, K. (1990). Paradox and groups. In J. Gillette & M. McCollom (Eds.), *Groups in context: A new perspective on group dynamics* (pp. 106–132). New York: University Press of America.

Bion, W. R. (1961). *Experiences in groups.* New York: Brunner-Routledge.

Bion, W. R. (1975). Selections from experiences in groups. In A. D. Colman & W. H. Bexton (Eds.), *Group relations reader 1* (pp. 11–20). Washington, DC: A. K. Rice Institute.

Blascovich, J., Mendes, W. B., Hunter, S., Lickel, B., & Kowai-Bell, N. (2001). Perceiver threat in social interactions with stigmatized others (Abstract). *Journal of Personality and Social Psychology, 80,* 253–267.

Brabeck, M., & Ting, K. (2000). Introduction. In M. Brabeck & K. Ting (Eds.), *Practicing feminist ethics in psychology* (pp. 3–15). Washington, DC: American Psychological Association.

Brown, A., & Mistry, T. (1994). Group work with "mixed membership" groups: Issues of race and gender. *Social Work With Groups, 17*(3), 5–21.

Carter, R. (2000). Perspectives on addressing cultural issues in organizations. In R. Carter (Ed.), *Addressing cultural issues in organizations: Beyond the corporate context* (pp. 3–18). Thousand Oaks, CA: Sage.

Cheng, W. D., Chase, M., & Gunn, R. (1998). Splitting and projective identification in multicultural group counseling. *Journal for Specialists in Group Work, 23*(4), 372–387.

Corey, M. S., & Corey, G. (2006). *Groups: Process and practice* (7th ed.). Belmont, CA: Brooks/Cole.

Cross, W. E. (1994). The psychology of nigrescence: Revising the cross model. In J. G. Ponterotto, J. M. Casas, L. A. Suzuki, & C. A. Alexander (Eds.), *Handbook of multicultural counseling* (pp. 93–122). Thousand Oaks, CA: Sage.

Dalal, F. (2002). *Race, colour and the process of racialization: New perspectives from group analysis, psychoanalysis and sociology.* New York: Brunner-Routledge.

D'Andrea, M., & Daniels, J. (2001). Expanding our thinking about white racism: Facing the challenge of multicultural counseling in the 21st century. In J. G. Ponterotto, J. M. Casas, L. A. Suzuki, & C. M. Alexander (Eds.), *Handbook of multicultural counseling* (pp. 289–310). Thousand Oaks, CA: Sage.

Davis, L. E., & Burnstein, E. (1981). Preference for racial composition of groups. *Journal of Psychology: Interdisciplinary and Applied, 109*(2), 293–301.

Dumas, R. G. (1985). Dilemmas of black females in leadership. In A. D. Colman & M. H. Geller (Eds.), *Group relations reader 2* (pp. 323–334). Jupiter, FL: A. K. Rice Institute.

Falicov, D. J. (1998). *Latino families in therapy: A guide to multicultural practice.* New York: Guilford Press.

Fanon, F. (1967). *Black skin, white masks.* New York: Grove Press.

Fenster, A. (1996). Group therapy as an effective treatment modality for people of color. *International Journal of Group Psychotherapy, 46*(3), 399–416.

Forsyth, D. (1999). *Group dynamics* (3rd ed.). Belmont, CA: Wadsworth.

Fraher, A. L. (2004). Systems psychodynamics: The formative years of an interdisciplinary field at the Tavistock Institute. *History of Psychology, 7*(1), 65–84.

Frame, M. W., & Williams, C. B. (2005). A model of ethical decision making from a multicultural perspective. *Counseling and Values, 49*(3), 165–179.

Gastil, J. (1994). A definition and illustration of democratic leadership. *Human Relations, 47*(8), 953–975.

Gibbard, G. S., Hartman, J. J., & Mann, R. D. (1974). *Analysis of groups.* San Francisco: Jossey-Bass.

Gillette, J., & McCollom, M. (Eds.). (1995). *Groups in context: A new perspective on group dynamics.* Lanham, MD: University Press of America.

Gladding, S. T. (2003). *Group work: A counseling specialty* (4th ed.). Upper Saddle River, NJ: Merrill Prentice Hall.

Goldberger, N. R., & Veroff, J. B. (1995). *The culture and psychology reader.* New York: New York University Press.

Goode, E. (2007, June 17). Home alone: Does ethnic and racial diversity foster social isolation? Idea lab. *New York Times Magazine,* pp. 24–26.

Govorun, O., Fuegen, K., & Payne, B. K. (2006). Stereotypes focus defensive projection (Abstract). *Personality and Social Psychology Bulletin, 32*(6), 781–793.

Green, Z. G., & Molenkamp, R. (2005). *The BART system of group and organizational analysis: Boundaries, authority, role and task.* Retrieved May 14, 2005, from http://www.akriceinstitute.org/associations/8689/files/BART_Green_Molenkamp.pdf

Greene, L. R. (1999). Representations of the group-as-a-whole: Personality, situational, and dynamic determinants (Abstract). *Psychoanalytic Psychology, 16,* 403–425.

Hare, A. P. (1976). *Handbook of small group research* (2nd ed.). New York: Free Press.

Hayden, C., & Carr, A. W. (1993). Responsibility, accountability and ethics in organizations: Evaluation of Group Relations Conference consultants. In S. Cytrynbaum & S. Lee (Eds.), *Transformations in global and organizational systems: Changing boundaries in the 90's* (pp. 92–97) (Symposium proceedings). Rainier, WA: A. K. Rice Institute.

Hayden, C., & Molenkamp, R. J. (2004). The Tavistock primer II. In S. Cytrynbaum & D. Noumair (Eds.), *Group dynamics, organizational irrationality, and social complexity: Group relations reader 3* (pp. 135–156). Jupiter, FL: A. K. Rice Institute for the Study of Social Systems Series.

Heifetz, R. A. (1994). *Leadership without easy answers.* Cambridge, MA: Belknap Press of Harvard University.

Heifetz, R. A., & Linsky, M. (2002). *Leadership on the line: Staying alive through the dangers of leading.* Boston: Harvard Business School Press.

Heifetz, R. A., & Sinder, R. M. (1987). Political leadership: Managing the public's problem solving. In R. Reich (Ed.), *The power of public ideas* (pp. 179–203). Cambridge, MA: Ballinger.

Helms, J. E. (1990). *Black and white racial identity: Theory, research, and practice.* New York: Greenwood Press.

Helms, J. E. (1995). An update of Helms's white and people of color racial identity models. In J. G. Ponterotto, J. M. Casas, L. A. Suzuki, & C. M. Alexander (Eds.), *Handbook of multicultural counseling* (pp. 181–198). Thousand Oaks, CA: Sage.

Highlen, P. S. (1994). Racial/ethnic diversity in doctoral programs in psychology: Challenges for the twenty-first century. *Applied and Preventive Psychology, 3,* 91–108.

Hoggett, P., Mayo, M., & Miller, C. (2006). Relations of authority. *Journal of Organisational and Social Dynamics, 6*(2), 224–240.

Holvina, E. (2004). *Diversity, organizational change, and working with differences: What next?* (Commentaries, No. 3). Boston: Center for Gender in Organizations, Simmons College.

hooks, b. (2003). *Teaching community. A pedagogy of hope.* New York: Routledge.

Horowitz, L. (1985). Projective identification in dyads and groups. In A. D. Colman & M. H. Geller (Eds.), *Group relations reader 2* (pp. 21–35). Jupiter, FL: A. K. Rice Institute.

Ivey, A. E., Pederson, P. B., & Ivey, M. B. (2001). *Intentional group counseling: A microskills approach.* Belmont, CA: Brooks/Cole, Thomson.

Jackson, S. (1948, June 28). The lottery. *New Yorker.* Retrieved May 21, 2009, from http://www.classicshorts.com/stories/lotry.html

Jacobs, E. E., Masson, R. L., & Harvill, R. L. (2002). *Group counseling: Strategies and skills.* Pacific Grove, CA: Brooks/Cole.

Jordan, J. V. (2001). A relational-cultural model: Healing through mutual empathy. *Bulletin of the Menninger Clinic, 65,* 92–103.

Kernberg, O. F. (1976). *Object relations theory and clinical psychoanalysis.* New York: Aronson.

Kim, J. (1981). *Process of Asian-American identity development: A study of Japanese American women's perception of their struggle to achieve positive identities.* Unpublished doctoral dissertation, University of Massachusetts, Amherst.

Kitchner, K. S. (1984). Intuition, critical evaluation and ethical principles: The foundation for ethical decisions in counseling psychology. *The Counseling Psychologist, 12,* 43–55.

Klein, M. (1946). Notes on some schizoid mechanisms. *International Journal of Psychoanalysis, 27,* 99–110.

Kline, W. B. (2003). *Interactive group counseling and therapy.* Upper Saddle River, NJ: Merrill Prentice Hall.

Kluckhohn, F. R., & Strodtbeck, F. L. (1961). *Variations in value orientation.* New York: Row, Peterson.

Kohut, H. (1980). Summarizing reflections. In A. Goldberg (Ed.), *Advances in self psychology* (pp. 473–554). New York: International Press.

Kovel, J. (1984). *White racism: A psychohistory.* New York: Columbia University Press.

Kuypers, B. C., Davies, D., & Hazewinkel, A. (1986). Developmental patterns in self-analytic groups. *Human Relations, 39*(9), 798–815.

LaFarge, V. S. (1990). Termination in groups. In M. McCollom & J. Gillette (Eds.), *Groups in context: A new perspective on group dynamics* (pp. 171–185). New York: Addison-Wesley.

Lahav, Y. (2009). Exploring Jewish identity, belonging and leadership through the lens of group relations: Reflections and challenges. In E. Aram, R. Baxter, & A. Nutkevitch (Eds.), *Adaptation and innovation: Theory, design and role-taking in group relations conferences and their applications* (pp. 163–177). London: Karnac Books.

Lakin, M. (1999). Morality in group and family therapies: Multiperson therapies and the 1992 ethics code. In D. N. Bersoff (Ed.), *Ethical conflicts in psychology* (2nd ed., pp. 133–137). Washington, DC: American Psychological Association.

Lawrence, G. W., Bain, A., & Gould, L. (1996). The fifth basic assumption. *Free Associations,* *6*(37), 28–55.

Lewin, K. (1951). *Field theory in social science.* New York: Harper & Row.

Li, J., Karakowsky, L., & Siegel, J. P. (1999). The effects of proportional representation on intragroup behavior in mixed-race decision-making groups. *Small Group Research,* *30*(3), 259–279.

MacKenzie, K. (1990). *Introduction to time-limited group psychotherapy.* Washington, DC: American Psychiatric Press.

Magee, J. C., Gruenfeld, D. H., Keltner, D. J., & Galinsky, A. D. (2004). Leadership and the psychology of power. In D. M. Messick & R. M. Krammer (Eds.), *The psychology of leadership: New perspectives and research* (pp. 275–293). Mahwah, NJ: Lawrence Erlbaum.

McCollom, M. (1990). Group formation: Boundaries, leadership, and culture. In J. Gillette & M. McCollom (Eds.), *Groups in context: A new perspective on group dynamics* (pp. 34–38). Lanham, MD: University Press of America.

McPherson, J. M., & Smith-Lovin, L. (1987). Homophily in voluntary organizations: Status distance and the composition of face-to-face groups. *American Sociological Review, 52*(3), 370–379.

McRae, M. B. (1994). Interracial group dynamics: A new perspective. *Journal for Specialists in Group Work, 19,* 168–174.

McRae, M. B. (2004). Class, race and gender issues in taking up the role of director: Training implications. In S. Cytrynbaum & D. Noumair (Eds.), *Group dynamics, organizational irrationality, and social complexity: Group relations reader III* (pp. 225–237). Jupiter, FL: A. K. Rice Institute.

McRae, M. B., & Johnson, S. D. (1991). Toward training for competence in multicultural counselor education. *Journal of Counseling and Development, 70,* 131–135.

McRae, M. B., Kwong, A., & Short, E. L. (2007). Racial dialogue among women: A group relations theory analysis. *Organizational & Social Dynamics, 7*(2), 211–234.

McRae, M. B., Orbe, L., Patel, S., & Hsu, M. (2008). *There is power in numbers.* Unpublished manuscript.

McRae, M. B., & Short, E. L. (2005). Racial-cultural training for group counseling and psychotherapy. In R. Carter (Ed.), *Handbook of racial-cultural psychology and counseling: Training and practice* (Vol. 2, pp. 135–147). Hoboken, NJ: Wiley.

Mennecke, B. E., Hoffer, J. A., & Wynn, B. E. (1992). The implications of group development and history for group support system theory and practice. *Small Group Research, 23*(4), 524–572.

Mendes, W. B., Blascovich, J., Lickel, B., & Hunter, S. (2002). Cardiovascular reactivity during social interactions with white and black men. *Personality and Social Psychology Bulletin, 28,* 939–952.

The Merriam-Webster dictionary online. (n.d.). Springfield, MA: Merriam-Webster. Retrieved October 31, 2008, from http://www.merriam-webster.com/dictionary/role

Miller, E. J. (1985). The politics of involvement. In A. D. Colman & M. H. Geller (Eds.), *Group relations reader 2* (pp. 383–398). Jupiter, FL: A. K. Rice Institute.

Miller, J. C. (1974). *Aspects of Tavistock consultation.* Unpublished dissertation, Yale University, New Haven, CT.

Mills, T. M. (1967). *The sociology of small groups.* Englewood Cliffs, NJ: Prentice Hall.

Mio, J. S., Barker-Hackett, L., & Tumambing, J. (2009). *Multicultural psychology: Understanding our diverse communities.* New York: McGraw-Hill.

Mitchell, S. (1988). *Relational concepts in psychoanalysis: An integration.* Cambridge, MA: Harvard University Press.

Morrison, T. (1992). *Playing in the dark: Whiteness and the literary imagination.* New York: Vintage Books.

Napier, R. W., & Gershenfeld, M. K. (1973). *Groups: Theory and experience.* Oxford, UK: Houghton Mifflin.

Obholzer, A. (1994). Authority, power and leadership: Contributions from group relations training. In A. Obholzer & V. Z. Roberts (Eds.), *The unconscious at work: Individual and organizational stress in the human services* (pp. 39–47). London: Routledge.

Parker, P. S. (2005). *Race, gender, and leadership.* Mahwah, NJ: Lawrence Erlbaum.

Pedersen, P. B. (1995). Culture-centered ethical guidelines for counselors. In J. G. Ponterotto, J. M. Casas, L. A. Suzuki, & C. M. Alexander (Eds.), *Handbook of multicultural counseling* (pp. 34–50). Thousand Oaks, CA: Sage.

Pedersen, P. B. (1997). The cultural context of the American Counseling Association Code of Ethics. *Journal of Counseling and Development, 76,* 23–76.

Ponterotto, J. G., & Pedersen, P. B. (1993). *Preventing prejudice: A guide for counselors and educators.* Newbury Park, CA: Sage.

Reed, G., & Noumair, D. (2000). The tiller of authority in a sea of diversity. In E. B. Klein, F. Gablenick, & P. Herr (Eds.), *Dynamic consultation in a changing workplace* (pp. 51–79). Madison, CT: Psychosocial Press.

Ridley, C. R., Liddle, M. C., Hill, C. L., & Li, L. C. (2001). Ethical decision making in multicultural counseling. In J. G. Ponterotto, J. M. Casas, L. A. Suzuki, & C. M. Alexander (Eds.), *Handbook of multicultural counseling* (2nd ed., pp. 165–188). Thousand Oaks, CA: Sage.

Rioch, M. (1985). Why I work as a consultant in the conferences of the A. K. Rice Institute. In A. D. Colman & M. H. Geller (Eds.), *Group relations reader 2* (pp. 365–381). Jupiter, FL: A. K. Rice Institute.

Rioch, M. J. (1975). The work of Wilfred Bion on groups. In A. D. Colman & W. H. Bexton (Eds.), *Group relations reader 1* (pp. 21–33). Washington, DC: A. K. Rice Institute.

Rosenbaum, S. C. (2004). Group-as-mother: A dark continent in group relations theory and practice. In S. Cytrynbaum & D. Noumair (Eds.), *Group dynamics, organizational irrationality, and social complexity: Group relations reader 3* (pp. 57–70). Jupiter, FL: A. K. Rice Institute.

Sampson, E. E. (1993). Identity politics: Challenges to psychology's understanding. *American Psychologist, 48*(12), 1219–1230.

Schultz, W. C. (1958). *Firo: A three-dimensional theory of interpersonal behavior.* New York: Holt, Rinehart & Winston.

Seligman, M. E. P. (2002). *Authentic happiness.* New York: Free Press.

Shapiro, E. L., & Ginzberg, R. (2002). Parting gifts: Termination rituals in group therapy. *International Journal of Group Psychotherapy, 52*(3), 319–336.

Shaw, J. B., & Barrett-Power, E. (1998). The effects of diversity on small work group processes and performance. *Human Relations, 51*(10), 1307–1325.

Short, E. L. (2007). Race, culture and containment in the formal and informal systems of group relations conferences. *Organizational & Social Dynamics, 7*(2), 156–171.

Slavson, S. R. (1956). Racial and cultural factors in group psychotherapy. *International Journal of Group Psychotherapy, 2,* 152–165.

Smith, G. (2001). Group development: A review of the literature and a commentary on future research directions. *Group Facilitation, 3,* 14–45.

Smith, K. K., & Berg, D. N. (1987). *Paradoxes in group life: Understanding conflict, paralysis, and movement in group dynamics.* San Francisco: Jossey-Bass.

Stock, D., & Thelen, H. A. (1958). *Emotional dynamics and group culture.* New York: New York University Press.

Sue, D. W., Arredondo, P., & McDavis, R. J. (1992). Multicultural counseling competencies and standards: A call to the profession. *Journal of Counseling & Development, 70,* 477–486.

Sue, D. W., Capodilupo, C. M., Torino, G. C., Bucceri, J. M., Holder, A. M. B., Nadal, K. L., et al. (2007). Racial microaggressions in everyday life: Implications for clinical practice. *American Psychologist, 62*(4), 271–286.

Sue, D. W., & Sue, D. (2008). *Counseling the culturally diverse: Theory and practice* (5th ed.). New York: Wiley.

Suzuki, L. A., Prevost, L., & Short, E. L. (2008). Multicultural issues and the assessment of aptitude. In L. A. Suzuki & J. G. Ponterotto (Eds.), *Handbook of multicultural assessment. Clinical, psychological, and educational applications* (pp. 490–519). San Francisco: Jossey-Bass.

Thomas, D. C. (1999). Cultural diversity and work group effectiveness: An experimental study. *Journal of Cross-Cultural Psychology, 30*(2), 242–263. Retrieved April 18, 2009, from http://jcc.sagepub.com/cgi/content/abstract/30/2/242

Tsui, A. S., & O'Reilly, C. A. (1989). Beyond simple demographic effects: The importance of demography in superior-subordinate dyads. *Academy of Management Journal, 32*(2), 402–423.

Tsui, P. (1997). The dynamics of cultural and power relations in group therapy. In E. Lee (Ed.), *Working with Asian Americans: A guide for clinicians* (pp. 354–363). New York: Guilford Press.

Tuckman, B. W. (1965). Developmental sequence in small groups. *Psychological Bulletin, 63*(6), 384–399.

Tuckman, B. W., & Jensen, M. C. (1977). Stages of small group development revisited. *Group and Organizational Studies, 2*(4), 419–427.

Turquet, P. M. (1974). Leadership: The individual and the group. In G. S. Gibbard, J. J. Hartman, & R. D. Mann (Eds.), *Analysis of groups* (pp. 349–371). San Francisco: Jossey-Bass.

Turquet, P. M. (1985). Leadership: The individual and the group. In A. D. Colman & M. H. Geller (Eds.), *Group relations reader 2* (pp. 71–87). Jupiter, FL: A. K. Rice Institute.

Viswanath, R. (2009). Identity, leadership, and authority: Experiences in application of group relations concepts for Dalit empowerment in India. In E. Aram, R. Baxter, & A. Nutkevitch (Eds.), *Adaptation and innovation: Theory, design and role-taking in group relations conferences and their applications* (pp. 179–195). London: Karnac Books.

Welfel, E. R. (2002). *Ethics in counseling and psychology: Standards, research, and emerging issues.* Pacific Grove, CA: Brook/Cole.

Welfel, E. R., & Kitchner, K. S. (1999). Introduction to special section: Ethics education—an agenda for the '90's. In D. N. Bersoff (Ed.), *Ethical conflicts in psychology* (2nd ed., pp. 133–137). Washington, DC: American Psychological Association.

Wells, L. (1985). The group-as-a-whole perspective and its theoretical roots. In A. D. Colman & M. H. Geller (Eds.), *Group relations reader 2* (pp. 109–126). Jupiter, FL: A. K. Rice Institute.

Wells, L. (1990). The group as a whole: A systematic socioanalytic perspective on interpersonal and group relations. In J. Gillette & M. McCollom (Eds.), *Groups in context: A new perspective on group dynamics* (pp. 49–85). New York: Addison-Wesley.

White, K. P. (2002). Surviving hating and being hated: Some personal thoughts about racism from a psychoanalytic perspective. *Contemporary Psychoanalysis, 38*(3), 401–422.

Wilson, G., & Hanna, M. (1990). *Groups in context.* New York: McGraw-Hill.

Wrenn, C. G. (1985). Afterward: The culturally encapsulated counselor revisited. In P. Pedersen (Ed.), *Handbook of cross-cultural counseling and therapy* (pp. 323–330). Westport, CT: Greenwood.

Yalom, I. D. (1995). *The theory and practice of group psychotherapy* (4th ed.). New York: Basic Books.

Index

About the Authors

Mary B. McRae is an associate professor of applied psychology in the Department of Applied Psychology, Steinhardt School of Culture, Education and Human Development at New York University. Presently, she teaches a course in Group Dynamics, Cross-Cultural Counseling, and Practicum in Counselor Training. Her scholarship involves a psychoanalytic and systemic study of authority and leadership in groups and organizations with a focus on issues of difference such as race, ethnicity, gender, social class, and culture. She is a licensed psychologist with a private practice. She is the founder of and has directed the annual experiential group relations conferences at New York University, educational laboratories created to study the life of the group and organization as they develop. They have been noted by the A. K. Rice Institute for the Study of Social Systems as the most innovative adaptation of the Tavistock model in working with issues of diversity. These conferences provide participants the opportunity to learn about authority and leadership as related to issues of difference in the "here and now" of the experience. She has worked as the associate director for group relations conferences at the Tavistock Clinic in London and as a consultant at other conferences in the United States, London, and Peru. She has been a member of an international team of consultants at the International Management Development business school, applying the Tavistock model to leadership and team building with managers and executives from international corporations. She is a fellow in the A. K. Rice Institute for the Study of Social Systems. She received her EdD in counseling psychology at Teachers College, Columbia University.

Ellen L. Short is currently an assistant professor at Long Island University, in the School of Education, Department of Human Development and Leadership, Counseling Programs. Her areas of specialization in teaching, scholarly research, and publishing are group dynamics focusing on race, ethnicity, gender, and culture; multicultural assessment of intelligence and aptitude tests; and substance use/abuse and high-risk behaviors among HIV-positive, heterosexual populations. She has served as a consultant at group relations conferences in the United States and internationally. She has also directed group relations conferences at Teachers College, Columbia University and New York University. She is a member of the A. K. Rice Institute for the Study of Social Systems and the New York Center for the Study of Groups, Organizations and Social Systems. She received her MA in counseling psychology from Northwestern University and her PhD in counseling psychology from New York University.

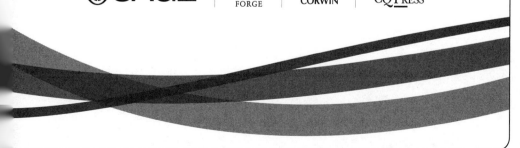